Brain Boot Camp

Terry Horne and Simon Wootton

D1390636

Hodder Education
338 Euston Road, London NW1 3BH
Hodder Education is an Hachette UK company

First published in UK 2012 by Hodder Education

www.hoddereducation.co.uk

Typeset by MPS Limited

Printed in Great Britain by CPI Cox & Wyman, Reading

Also available
in ebook

Also available in
ebook and audio

Also available as an ebook
and unabridged audio

Also available in
iphone app and audio

Acknowledgements

We are indebted to so many brain researchers (biologists, biochemists, neurologists, neuroscientists, dieticians, social workers and cognitive psychologists), and so many brain research centres specializing in ageing, that it is iniquitous to name only a few individuals and institutions.

That said, we especially acknowledge that much of our material was first researched with Roger Armstrong at LBS, University of Central Lancashire; Peter Checkland, Department of Systems Thinking and Practice, University of Lancaster; Tony Doherty, at the Centre for Social Enterprise, University of London; P. J. Howard at the Center for Cognitive Studies in Carolina, USA; Sayaka Mitsuhashi of the Okinawa Centenarian Centre; and David Gamon, Allen Bragdon, Ian Robertson, Guy Brown, Susan Greenfield, Jeff Victoroff, James Fixx, Rosemarie Janski, Zak Tan, Pam Ayres, Felix Dennis, Ian Deary, David Snowdon, Paul McKenna, Richard Templar, Sally Moon and Nathan Haselbayer of the International High IQ Society.

We are especially indebted to the Saunders-Brown Center on Aging in Kentucky, USA, Members of the Noetic Institute, UK, and the Institute of Brain and Aging at the University of California, Irvine.

This book is part of a long journey with many companions, usually for only part of the way. Part-way companions have included many research students, too many to mention. We thank them for their legacy of findings and good questions.

Contents

Meet the authors

Welcome to *Brain Boot Camp!*

We both started our adult lives as chemists: Terry specialized in the chemistry of complex organic molecules and Simon specialized in biochemistry. Later, while working for pharmaceutical companies such as Pfizer and Eli Lilly, Simon was very involved with pharmaceutical drugs that effectively changed the chemistry of the brain, in order to help manage moods or alleviate depression. At this point our career paths diverged. Simon moved into health services, both private and NHS, while Terry became interested in managers and how they thought about solving problems, taking decisions and making plans.

Happily, some years later our career paths converged once more. Simon returned to university and, based on his research, together we wrote *Strategic Thinking*, one of Kogan Page's bestselling books on strategy. *Strategic Thinking* has been translated into Chinese, Spanish and Russian, and a third edition was published in 2010. With another research student, Tony Doherty, there followed *Managing Public Services – Implementing Changes: A Thoughtful Approach to the Practice of Management*, a bestselling book for Routledge.

In the meantime, the number of students going to university had risen from 1 in 10 school leavers, to 4 in 10 school leavers. Many of these additional students had neither the thinking skills nor the cognitive capacity to study properly for a degree. How could thinking skills and cognitive capacity be developed?

We put our heads together – literally – and began to think about the brain as if it were a chemical factory. In this we had support from Professor Susan Greenfield, one of the world's leading neuroscientists. Together, we produced what Susan Greenfield has since described as 'the world's most advanced models of the way the brain thinks'.

There are two important implications of our models of the way the brain thinks. First, Simon knew that the chemical reactions which carry your thoughts through your brain can be made to go faster and further by changing the general chemical conditions in your brain; he also knew that you can learn to control those chemical conditions by choosing what you eat, what you do and how you feel. We had discovered that your effective intelligence was determined by your choices, and not just by your genes.

Second, Terry was fascinated by Susan Greenfield's idea of neuromodulation. This was the realization that, once one of your thoughts had caused a particular neural pathway to be run, this changed the residual chemicals left along the neural pathway. Those chemicals then made it easier for that neural pathway to be run again. We had discovered that the very act of thinking strengthens your ability to think. It is now possible to design thinking activities which connect up different parts of your brain and which can then strengthen those connections.

The brain training books which we have written for managers, students, adults and the 50+ are the result of a happy convergence of biochemistry and cognitive science. This current book, *Brain Boot Camp*, is for everyone.

We hope you have fun and enjoy the benefits it will bring you.

Terry Horne and Simon Wootton

Introduction: Your amazing brain

Train your brain!

Your brain chemically fires off about a million neurons a second. It constantly changes and develops its power and plasticity, from age minus 9 months to plus 90 years. Most of what we know about your brain has been discovered in your lifetime. Much of it was discovered in the last few years!

The more we train our brains, the higher our performance becomes and remains. The used brain has a higher ratio of synaptic connections to neurons. The neural nerve growth factor (NGF) is actually released by the process of thinking. This, in turn, promotes the thickening of the myelin insulation around the axons of the connected neurons.

In this book of 'addictive fun', each of the 14 brain training 'circuits' has 15 puzzles that will exercise different combinations of your mental muscles. The 15 exercises are then followed by one cryptic crossword which will give you practice in applying your new thinking skills.

For some people, doing regular circuits in the gym is the best way to improve their performance in the field. For others, 'the game is the best coach'. You can try either the series of 15 puzzles, or the cryptic crossword, or both. Since each circuit is composed of the same mix of some easy, and some difficult puzzles, your score should improve between Circuit 1 and Circuit 14. In the case of the cryptic cross word puzzles, you should find that you can do them more easily as you work your way through from Circuit 1 to Circuit 14. That is because the puzzles are of similar levels of difficulty and you will get better with practice.

Here's the theory...

Neuroscientists were prompted to look for evidence of continued brain development in adult brains by the US research psychologist Mark Rosenzweig's observations of mice. Young mice set problems or puzzles to solve added new neurons at rate of 4,000 a day, compared with 2,400 a day in a control group that were not set problems or puzzles to solve. Not only was the rate of production of new neurons 66-per-cent faster, the new neurons had more dendrites and longer axons (see the next section for explanation of these). That is to say, Rosenzweig's problem-solving mice were each day developing neurons that were better equipped to make the interconnections that support intelligent behaviour and increased reserves of cognitive capacity.

Even more exciting for brain trainers was Rosenzweig's discovery, since replicated by other researchers, that the same effect was found in old mice. In the old mice, many of the new brain cells appeared near the hippocampus – a vital centre for directing new memory information and new learning.

The neuroscientist Elizabeth Gould, at Princeton University, was able to separate the developments caused by purely mental exercises from developments caused by physical exercise. The mental brain training had the most powerful effect – more powerful even than physical exercise and diet. The effects were enhanced when the activities were carried out in social situations, rather than in isolation.

Active engagement and challenge appear to be necessary for improved mental fitness. A useful analogy might be pushing yourself beyond your comfort zone, by using a heart rate monitor to do aerobic exercise.

When undertaking the 14 circuits, try not to skip a puzzle. If you find it hard, discuss it with someone else. Be persistent. The churning is the learning – especially if done aloud and especially if done with another person.

Within each of the circuits, we have included some puzzles that will specifically target the left side of your brain. We have done this because this stimulates centres that hold positive emotions. We know that elevated mood enhances mental performance and will generate the motivation for you to finish the circuit! PET scans show that you laugh on the left side of your brain (and cry on the right).

Before getting down to the hard work, however, we'll first of all take a look at the thing we are aiming to train – the brain itself. We will discover exactly why brain training works and how people of *every* age can benefit from it. Moreover, just as in the gym where an understanding of how the body works – the muscles, ligaments and so on – can be crucial, we train our brains most effectively when we grasp how this extraordinary organ functions.

Electrical v chemical brain

From the 1970s onwards, we have been trying to imagine what happens inside your brain when you try to think. We and others have been trying to help students, teachers, managers, therapists, social workers and public sector workers to learn to think more effectively about the kinds of decisions they need to take, the kinds of problems they need to solve, and the kinds of plans they need to make.

At first, we were helped by the then prevailing model of 'brain-as-computer'.

Popular in the 1970s and 1980s, this model argued that it was useful to view the brain as computer *hardware*, and the mind as the computer *software*. The idea is beguiling and there are many useful parallels. For example, when you turn off a computer, the software cannot work. Your brain needs a reliable supply of energy or it will suffer rather like your computer suffers. Also, a computer needs background software – for example, the software that periodically clears 'garbage' and consolidates memory files. Your brain is the same – it has autonomic activities that operate when you are asleep. Likewise, just because a computer is turned on, it doesn't mean that all the software programs are running. Some programs need to be requested explicitly. In the brain, this 'requesting' is called metacognative thinking and involves the part of the brain called the frontal cerebral cortex. Many of the exercises in this book will help you to exploit the frontal cortex of your brain, so that you can learn to direct your own thinking. This part of the brain is very underdeveloped in young adults but matures with age.

Despite the usefulness of the electrical model, we kept finding aspects of the ways our students were thinking that it failed to explain. In 1997, Susan Greenfield published *The Human Brain: A Guided Tour* in which she described how products of the mind, such as ideas and images, could cause *chemical* changes in the brain. Her model of the brain as a chemical factory liberated us from the straitjacket of our computer model. Suddenly, we could better understand the successes and the difficulties we were having with our students. Her neurochemical approach gave us ways to understand what we already knew.

At last, we could understand why, for many students, learning almost anything seemed to increase their capacity to learn, irrespective of the subject matter. For other students, lots of repetitions of relatively simple thinking tasks seemed to produce marked improvements in their capacity to think. This supported our emerging view that thinking was a combination of ten or so contributory skills (Figure 1).

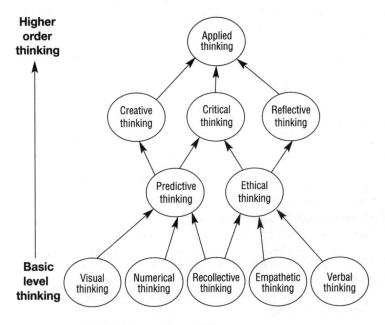

Figure 1 The hierarchy of thinking skills (Horne and Wootton, 2010).

Although logic (deductive and inductive) remains the backbone of clear thinking, it is a necessary, but not sufficient, condition for thinking at its best. Parts of the brain other than the frontal cerebral cortex have a role to play if thinking is to be first class.

The parts of your brain that control visual images, and the parts of your brain that empathize with the likely thoughts and feelings of other people, can work in concert with the parts of your brain that hold different facets of your memory. All these different parts of your brain can help the frontal lobe of your cortex to take a more logical decision or to make a more rational plan. Susan Greenfield's work gave us confidence to extend our ideas on combination thinking and to devise brain training exercises that involve the simultaneous use of different parts of the brain.

The structure and composition of the brain

If you want to train your brain, it can be helpful to find out something about the structure and composition of the brain you are seeking to train.

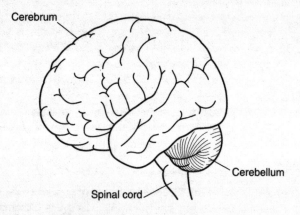

Figure 2 The human brain (taken from Horne and Wootton, 2010).

Inside your skull, your brain has the consistency of a sloppy undercooked egg. It has no moving parts. It is surrounded by a colourless fluid (CSF), which is circulating constantly. CSF contains mainly salt and sugar.

The brain itself is wrinkled and creamy in colour. Although it would fit into the palm of your hand, it is as heavy as three bags of sugar. The brain has two halves and looks rather like a small cauliflower whose stalk tapers to become the top of your spinal cord. The back of the cauliflower overhangs the stalk slightly. The overhang is called the cerebellum. The main part is called the cerebrum.

If you turn the brain over, you will see distinct regions that occur in pairs, so that the underside of the brain appears to be symmetrical about a central line running from the front to the back of the brain.

DIFFERENT JOBS FOR DIFFERENT BITS OF THE BRAIN

Your cerebral cortex is divided into about 50 different bits, many of which have a definite specialized function. In some parts of the cortex, towards the back for instance (the posterior parietal cortex), the distinction between the areas is more blurred. The posterior parietal cortex handles many sensations – sound, sight, touch and movement.

The frontal lobes of a mature brain become active when they are asked to empathize, make predictions, or tackle problems that involve planning, complex decisions or creative thinking. Teenagers, or young adults under 25, often struggle with these kinds of thinking tasks. Often, the development of this frontal area of their cerebral cortex lags behind the bushing of the dendrites (see below) in the back of their brain, which is preoccupied with sensation and stimulation. Until the development of their frontal lobes catches up, young people are usually reluctant to volunteer verbal information, and they can appear to be anti-social and to have 'heads like sieves' when it comes to remembering things.

NEURONS – THE BUILDING BLOCKS OF THE BRAIN

Neurons have a squat, blob-like body called a soma, about 0.04 mm across. The soma sprouts tiny branches called dendrites. Commonly, neurons appear elongated, with dendrites at either end, sometimes on the end of a long, thin fibre called an axon. The axon is commonly two to three times longer than the body of the neuron, though spinal neurons can trail axons a metre long. So, squat somas, with stubby dendrite branches and long thin tails – these are your neurons. Neurons are the building blocks of your constantly developing intelligence.

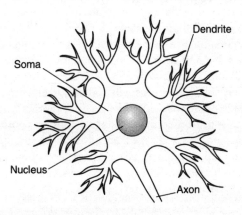

Figure 3 The nerve cell and branches (taken from Horne and Wootton, 2010).

DENDRITES AND AXONS – WHAT DO THEY DO?

The dendrites are receiving stations for chemical messages sent out by neighbouring neurons. The chemical messages converge down the dendrites into the neuron body. If the signals are strong enough, the neuron will generate an electrical charge, which will be conducted along the axon towards the dendrites of neighbouring neurons.

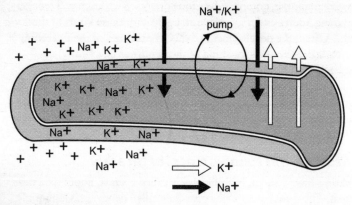

Figure 4 The dendrite.

The charges are carried either by positively charged sodium, potassium or calcium cations, or by negatively charged chloride anions. The charged anions and cations cannot normally pass through the fatty inter-layers of the neuron wall. However, an accumulation of negatively charged ions on the inside of the neuron wall will attract, rather like a magnet, ions and proteins of opposite charge to the outside of the neuron wall, thereby generating a difference in potential across the cell wall. This potential difference can be measured in millivolts. When the potential difference reaches about 80 millivolts, channels open through the neuron walls, to allow positively charged ions (usually sodium) to enter the neuron to neutralize the negative charges on the inside of the neuron. When the charge inside the neuron becomes about 20 millivolts positive, then potassium ions, positively charged, are allowed out through the wall of the neuron, until a negatively charged state is restored inside the neuron. All this happens in a thousandth of a second.

The direction of transmission of the electrical charges, and the speeds of the transmission, are determined by the directions and condition of the axons. If the axon is already connected to a dendrite of another neuron, then that predetermines the direction taken by the charge. If the axon is surrounded by a thick sheath of healthy myelin insulation, the transmission will be fast and accurate. Because you often wish to minimize the delay between one thought and the next, or between thought and action, chemical charges will hustle down your axons at about 400 km/hour, as long as the myelin insulation on your axons are in good enough condition. What happens when the electrically charged chemicals hit the synaptic gap between the end of the axon and the dendrite of a neighbouring neuron?

BRIDGING THAT GAP

With the advent of electron microscopes, which have magnification factors of over 10,000, chemicals can be detected in the synaptic gap. Among the chemicals detected in the synaptic gap are many differently shaped acetylcholine derivatives. These acetylcholine molecules belong to a general class of brain chemicals known as neurotransmitters.

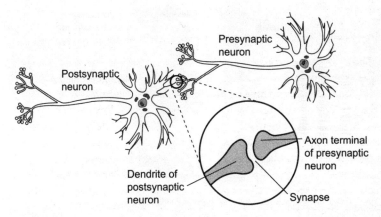

Figure 5 The synapse.

The more frequently electrically charged chemicals arrive at the end of the axon, the more often acetylcholine neurotransmitters can be seen launching themselves into the water in the synaptic gap. The small size of the neurotransmitters enables them to diffuse very quickly across the salty water that surrounds the axons and dendrites. They cross the gap in less than a millisecond, but how do they know which dendrite to choose?

Each neurotransmitter swimming across the gap is like a jigsaw piece, looking for a dendrite with a receptor molecule of exactly the right shape to make a perfect fit. Once the neurotransmitter finds and locks onto a right-fitting receptor, this signals to the channel in the wall of the second neuron to admit a charged chemical. An accumulation of charged chemicals moves down the dendrites of the second neuron into the cell body and out along the axon of the second neuron to the edge of the next synaptic gap, where it stares across the water at a third neuron. This is going on inside your amazing chemical brain a million times a second!

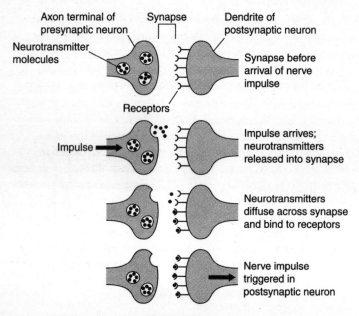

Figure 6 Synaptic transmissions (taken from Horne and Wootton, 2010).

While neurotransmitters like serotonin, dopamine and even acetylcholine frequently get a mention in popular accounts of brain chemistry, there is another neurotransmitter that rarely gets a mention. It is called glutamate and is important for memory. However, glutamate can also cause neuron death. Too much glutamate appears to overexcite receiving neurons (by causing too much calcium to flood in), causing death by excitotoxicity. Excitotoxicity is one of the main causes of death in strokes, head injuries and Alzheimer's disease.

The developing brain

It is the quantity (and quality) of your neuron connections, not the number or weight of your neurons, that appears to determine your cognitive capacity and your mental performance. This has changed our view on the way the adult brain continues to develop. Work by Robert Siegler, at Carnegie University (USA) in the late 1990s, on embryos, babies, pre-school infants, teenagers, adults and seniors, indicates that brain development is ongoing throughout your life and that there is no cut-off in the development of your intelligence or in the development of your thinking skills (look back at Figure 1).

Every year, the young adult brain shrinks and loses weight. This loss is now thought to be due more to a loss of weight by individual neurons, rather than to the loss of individual neurons themselves. Losses can be compensated for by learning things, almost anything, because learning almost anything increases the density of your synaptic connections. Also, by applying, reciting or repeating what you have learned, or thought about, you increase the thickness of the myelin insulation around the axons of your neurons. This thicker myelin insulation results in quicker and clearer electrical transmission through your brain and more secure storage of information. Thicker myelination improves the recall of your memories and the speed and accuracy of your thinking. The brain training activities in this book have been designed to increase the number of synaptic connections in your brain and to thicken the myelin insulation of your axons. This process, whereby the act of thinking chemically modifies the route along which the thought has been chemically transmitted, is called neuromodulation.

THE YOUNG ADULT BRAIN

The brain growth spurt that begins when you are a teenager starts at the back of your brain, heightening your awareness and sensitivity to sounds, lights, tastes and touch. Because development in the middle of the brain comes later, young adults often do not feel in control of their emotional reactions and impulses. Young adults often feel awkward or clumsy. But the lag in the development of their frontal cortex is the biggest disability for young adults. This frontal cortex is involved in reasoning, planning, predicting and decision making. Small wonder the behaviour of many young adults often seems unreasonable and lacking in direction and to have little regard for risk and consequence. According to the US psychiatrist Jay Giedd, reporting in 2004, this is because many young adults lack the ability of the mature brain to reason, to decide, and to assess risk and consequence.

THE MATURE BRAIN

Your brain can start to show a net loss of neurons if you drink alcohol or use certain other drugs. Don't panic! You can still preserve and improve your IQ and the intelligence of your behaviour. This is because many of the thinking skills that contribute to intelligent behaviour (Figure 1 again) improve as you get older, as long as you learn to apply them explicitly when you need them. This kind of thinking – called 'applied thinking' – produces more intelligent behaviour. It is a mistaken belief that memory necessarily deteriorates with age. In fact, your ability to recall early knowledge and experiences gets better. This is because recall benefits from repetition and you are more likely to have repeated a particular recall the older you get. On the other hand, what is likely to deteriorate from the age of 50 is the speed at which you can form new memories. New information processing often does slow down. We have included brain training exercises that mitigate this.

Repairing the brain

It is fortunate that brain training can repair brain damage, because all of our brains are at risk from, for example:

▶ *extended grief, depression, low mood or pessimism*
▶ *alcohol*
▶ *oxygen depletion and toxins, due to lack of exercise*
▶ *poor diet and the additives in processed food*
▶ *all manner of environmental threats*
▶ *raised blood pressure, often alcohol- or stress-related*
▶ *lack of stimulation or lack of conversational relationships.*

Mental performance does not inevitably decline with age, if you stay healthy. While it is true that certain diseases can lower mental performance, if you build up sufficient reserves of spare cognitive capacity such diseases will have less or no effect. The brain training circuits in this book can help you to create reserves of spare cognitive capacity. People who do not use their brains productively tend to drag down the average scores for older adults, and so obscure the high and increasing scores of those older people who use their brains productively.

Edward Coffey, of the Henry Ford Foundation, reported that adults aged 65 to 90 who used their brains actively, continued to perform well with no signs of loss of memory or reason, despite their MRI scans showing shrinkage in the size of their brains. In 2002, Quartz reported on a famous study of 4,000 nuns. This study was commenced by David Snowdon in Kentucky in 1986. The study is particularly interesting because all the nuns have very similar lifestyles, but some continue to teach and to be mentally active, and some don't. The nuns who continue to be mentally active are currently living, on average, four years longer, and their brain autopsies show, on average, 40 per cent more synapses and thicker myelin insulation on their axons. So, thinking helps you to live longer and thinking helps your brain to keep getting better and better. Thinking adds years to your life as well as life to your years.

We now understand *why* we should train our brains... Let's get down to the training itself. We can promise it will be hard work, fruitful and fun, too!

The circuits

Before you begin the brain boot camp, here are a few reminders and pointers about how you should approach the circuits:

The brain training workout has two components: a **series of 14 blocks of exercises** (or circuits), and 14 **cryptic crosswords**. You can try either the series of exercises, or the cryptic crosswords, or both. Since each circuit is composed of the same mix of exercises, some easy and some difficult, then your score should improve between Circuit 1 and Circuit 14. In the case of the 14 cryptic crossword puzzles, you should find that you can do them more easily as you work your way through from Circuit 1 to Circuit 14. That is because the puzzles are of similar levels of difficulty and you will get better with practice.

Solving a **cryptic crossword** simultaneously involves traffic between many different areas of your brain as you try to:

▶ use logic

▶ recollect obscure bits of general knowledge

▶ make creative associations between the bits you remember

▶ count letters and spaces

▶ hold several possibilities in your short-term memory

▶ decide on the most likely possibilities

▶ analyse the best way to crosscheck your decision, *and, finally,*

▶ manage your motivation and frustration!

Cryptic crosswords don't just test your brain power – more importantly, the attempts you make to solve the cryptic clues leave **new neural traces** and **connections** in your brain. These new neural connections create new cognitive capacity that improves your performance on other thinking tasks and also helps to protect your improved performance against disease by creating reserve cognitive capacity.

All these separate aspects of your brain development are intensified if you do, or discuss, the puzzle with **another person**. Hence the brain developing power of **paired learning**, or of acting as a 'critical friend', or of being a 'thoughtful companion'. So, please take every opportunity to work on brain training exercises with someone else.

Try not to skip a puzzle if you find it hard. Discuss it with someone else. Be persistent. The churning is the learning – especially if done aloud and especially if done with another person. Professor Timiras found that mechanical memory training, done in isolation, produced only a short-term gain in overall mental performance. The gain faded unless there was constant repetition, recall and reinforcement.

Now, turn either to the first circuit – or to the first cryptic crossword (these are located after each circuit). Keep a note of how many of the circuit puzzles, or cryptic clues, you can solve. You will, we promise, progressively be able to solve more of the problems, more quickly.

Above all, have fun!

Circuit 1

The Titanic was built by professionals, the Ark was built by amateurs.

Terry Horne

Q1 *Are you afraid to start? Make your way from Fear to Hope, changing one letter at a time.*

HOPE

_____

_____

_____

_____

FEAR

Q2 *When does coffee taste like soil?*

Q3 *The letters A, B, C, D, E, F each represent a different digit in the range 0–8. Which letters represent which numbers? (There are hints and clues below.)*

A	+	B	=	A
C	+	A	=	D
D	+	C	=	EB
EB	+	D	=	ED
ED	+	EB	=	AD
AD	+	ED	=	CA
CA	+	AD	=	DF
DF	+	CA	=	EEB
EEB	+	DF	=	EGF

> **Hint:** First line gives B = 0; third line gives E = 1 since 2 digits cannot add to 20; seventh line is 42 + 26 = 68).

> **Clue:** C = 4, A = 2, D = 6

Q4 The only Bond girl to appear in three Bond films, in 1974, 1983, 1985, now divides her continuing career between the USA and her native Sweden.

_ _ _ _ / _ _ _ _ _ _ (4, 5)

Hint: Surname belonging to someone from Eden.

Q5 Can you get yourself up from being idle to become the academic stars at a university (one letter at a time)?

_____
_____
_____
_____

LAZE

Hint: Start in a daze get it finished.

Q6 Every block in this pyramid contains a number which is the sum of the two on which it rests. What are the missing numbers?

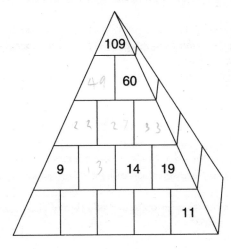

Q7 *Complete the Sudoku.*

			3			8		1
				5	6	7	3	
4	3	7		9	8	2	6	
1		3				5	7	8
6	4	8	5			3		
	9						4	2
3	6	1		2	5			
	8	4			1			6
9	7			8	4	1		3

On every circuit, questions 8, 9 and 10 will be about numbers – their significance in nature, mathematics, science, religion, mythology, art or history.

Q8 _ _ _ _ _ _ _ _ _ *tons of TNT is used as a measure of explosive power.*

Hint: As in a 3-megaton bomb (from Greek 'mega' = very large).

Q9 *Jesus is said to have sent out _ _ disciples, and this number of wives await in heaven.*

Q10 *The _ _ s brought boom and bust to Wall Street, and brought fascism, brilliant jazz, penicillin, cars, TV, flights and votes for women. The era of James Joyce, Franz Kafka, George Bernard Shaw, T. S. Eliot, Al Jolson, Charlie Chaplin, Buster Keaton and Houdini.*

Hint: It is the most common 'score' and two of them combine to give perfect vision.

When you have worked out the titles of the next four films, try to rent, buy or borrow and watch them. They are all brain workouts. They all involve emotional, visual and verbal thinking, plus either logic to aid your critical thinking, or humour to aid your creativity.

Q11 After tempting fate by numbering it 13, the NASA control room became the brain of the United States, trying to work out how to get Tom Hanks back.

☐ ☐ ☐ ☐ ☐ ☐

Hint: Aphrodite's friend?

Q12 A new direction in settling accounts.

☐ ☐ ☐ ☐ ☐ ☐ ☐ ☐ ☐ ☐ ☐ ☐

Hint: Not backwards.

Q13 A definite start to one who plays ivories (black and white not Merchant).

☐ ☐ ☐   ☐ ☐ ☐ ☐ ☐ ☐ ☐

Hint: Musician.

Q14 Beginning gravely and ending saying a shortened hello, he needed a connector of words in the middle to free his country.

☐ ☐ ☐ ☐ ☐ ☐

Hint: Peace-loving Hindu, freed an Asian subcontinent.

Q15

is to A, B or C?

A   B   C

Hint: Mirrors.

How did you get on?

Score 3 for each correct answer.

Score an extra 3 points if you did not use the Hints.

Enter your total here ☐

1 in 2 people can expect to score 10 or less when they start.

1 in 40 people can expect to improve their score to 70+.

Cryptic tip 1

Every cryptic crossword clue gives you at least two ways to find the answer.

One is to find the synonym for part of the clue, i.e. a word meaning the same.

The other way is to find the answer through a play on the words that are to be found in the rest of the clue.

For example:

Male goose is all mixed up in danger. (6)

We find the answer twice: once because a male goose is a gander; and the second time because 'gander' is to be got from the letters of 'danger' all mixed up.

The **first task** is to spot and separate the word (or few words) for which the synonym is required. In these cryptic tips we will put these in upper case: MALE GOOSE. Normally, several possible synonyms might be the answer. Untangling the play on the remaining words in the clue will normally reduce the number of possibilities to only one possible answer. This will be confirmed when the answer fits in with the cross letters from other clues in the crossword.

The **second task** is to spot the instructional words that tell us what kind of game is to be played with some of the remaining words in the clue. In the example above, the cryptic operation was an anagram of 'danger', and this was signalled by the words 'all mixed up'. There are many different ways of signalling a particular operation. For example, anagrams may be indicated by words like 'confused by', 'rearranged', 'all shook up', 'stirring'. The possibilities are many, and spotting them becomes easier with experience and practice. When giving cryptic tips, we will show the operation in italics: *all mixed up*.

The **third task** is to identify the words on which the cryptic operation is to take place. In our cryptic tips we will embolden these words: **danger**. So a cryptic clue has three important parts:

THE WORD(S) FOR WHICH A SYNONYM IS REQUIRED

+

a cryptic operation

+

the word(s) on which the cryptic operation is to take place.

Cryptic crossword 1

ACROSS

2. The loans get mixed up at the hairdressers (5)
4. 'It's Ben about a vegetable' (4)
6. The thirteenth friend of Aphrodite is misspelt in apology (7)
7. An uncertain approach to Dante produced music that was slow moving (7)
11. Goosey is in danger (6)
13. What nudity creates can be messy (6)
15. Within lust I erased sounds of crying (4)
17. Because it was stabled incorrectly it exploded (7)
18. Specimen maples were chopped up in error (6)

DOWN

1. Indian guru began gravely and ended saying a shortened hello, needing a connector of words in the middle to free his country (6)
2. You can find a solid fuel replacement in a lost over (5)
3. You break the chain to go there for all the tea (5)
5. To get your own back in Geneva (6)
8. An error in pouring made a candle lighter (5)
9. Burned by the sun, it somehow lightens the load (9)
10. Caution alters sale (7)
12. Editor gives rise to a commotion (6)
14. Although he displayed flair, he was weak (5)
16. Use a gas to make the filling for a hot dog (7)

Hint: 'Sounds like' = the synonym indicated 'sounds like' or rhymes with the answer.

Circuit 2

I live in a place where people still point at aeroplanes.

Terry Horne

Q1 *Using only 0, 1, 2, 3 or 4 only once in each line, complete the grid, so that each vertical, horizontal and diagonal has one, and only one, of each of the numbers 0, 1, 2, 3, 4.*

1	3	4	0	2
4	0	2	1	3
2	1	3	4	0
3	4	0	2	1
0	2	1	3	4

Q2 *How could you make sure a ghost was horizontal?*

Q3 *Fill in the numbers in the bottom row.*

6	6	12	18
30	48	78	126
204	330	534	

Hint: Numbers get bigger from left to right, and progress similarly one to the next.

Clue: Last number > 800.

26

Q4 *The world's first black supermodel. A Cosmopolitan cover girl in 1976, she is now president of a worldwide business empire.*

__ __ __ __ __ __ __ / __ __ __ __ __ __ __ (7, 7)

Hint: First find the hills in Hollywood and then a famous doctor.

Q5 *The protein in eggs is so good for your brain you can rise to be a poet.*

_____ ?

_____

_____

_____

_____

EGGS

Hint: Full of electrifying energy you can make mistakes and hear that you will be behind, before you become like Shakespeare.

Q6 *Every block in this pyramid contains a number which is the sum of the two on which it rests. What are the missing numbers?*

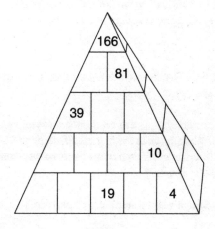

Q7 *Complete the Sudoku.*

1			6	5			8	9
			8		9	1		6
		9	1	3	7	2	4	
			3			9		
	3		5		6			
		6	2	8	1	3	5	7
	6		7	1	8			3
	9	1			2	8		
8		5			3	6	2	1

On every circuit, questions 8, 9 and 10 will be about numbers – their significance in nature, mathematics, science, religion, mythology, art or history.

Q8 *After working well on the farm, George decided to write another book in 1948 and digitally reworked that year.*

_ _ _ _

Hint: He not only wrote when down on the farm, but when down and out in Paris (and London).

Q9 *Sexual position, _ _ was the number of votes required to elect George Washington as the first president of the USA and is the record number of children born to one mother, Shuya, who was Russian (in a hurry?).*

Hint: Two of Shuya's children died, 67 survived.

28

Q10 To talk __ __ to the dozen is to talk very fast and busily, leading perhaps to this number of nervous breakdowns (Rolling Stones). By the Second World War, the average age of a combat soldier was 26, but in the Vietnam War it fell to this number. In 1642, King Charles I rejected this number of propositions for transferring power from the throne to Parliament, thereby precipitating the English Civil War.

Hint: The last year you were a teenager.

When you have worked out the titles of the next four films, try to rent, buy or borrow and watch them. They are all brain workouts. They all involve emotional, visual and verbal thinking, plus either logic to aid your critical thinking or humour to aid your creativity.

Q11 Did this society meet in a morgue? Membership definitely confined to bards, perhaps in water.

☐ ☐ ☐ ☐ ☐   ☐ ☐ ☐ ☐

Hint: *Carpe diem* – another Robin Williams triumph.

Q12 Floated on precious water.

☐ ☐   ☐ ☐ ☐ ☐ ☐ ☐   ☐ ☐ ☐ ☐

Hint: Henry Fonda in his golden age.

Q13 A sadomasochistic study penned by feathers.

☐ ☐ ☐ ☐ ☐ ☐

Hint: Begins with a long wait and does not end in heaven.

Q14 Not warmed up before the race.

☐ ☐ ☐ ☐ ☐   ☐ ☐ ☐ ☐ ☐ ☐ ☐

Hint: Hilarious exploits of an Olympic bobsleigh team short of practice in the West Indies.

Q15 *Three surviving soldiers divided their remaining bullets equally between them. After they had each fired four bullets, the total number of bullets left was the same as they each had after they had divided them. What was the original number remaining before they were equally divided between them?*

Hint: If the total originally divided was T, then each had 1/3 of T. Therefore T/3 = Total left after shooting 3 × 4 bullets.

How did you get on?

Score 3 for each correct answer.

Score an extra 3 points if you did not use the Hints.

Enter your total here

1 in 2 people can expect to score 10 or less when they start.

1 in 40 people can expect to improve their score to 70+.

Cryptic tip 2

It can be helpful to compare normal crossword clues with cryptic clues. Here are some comparisons:

Answer	Normal clue	Cryptic clue
Mamba	Venomous reptile	*Shortly* **mother** took **academic manager** to see a VENOMOUS REPTILE
Brainy	Intelligent	INTELLIGENT **female support I** take *briefly* to **New York**
Brawn	Strength	**Pressed beef** *makes* you STRONG

Note how 'shortly' or 'briefly' often indicates that abbreviations are involved. In the above examples, 'briefly to New York' = NY and 'shortly mother took academic manager' = Ma + MBA.

These examples illustrate how the normal clue is always somewhere in the cryptic clue – usually near the front or the end of the wordplay part. This makes cryptic clues easier to solve than apparently more straightforward normal crossword clues, because cryptic clues are normal clues plus extra information to help you uncover the synonym that is the answer.

Cryptic crossword 2

ACROSS

5. Mixed up loves remove the problem (5)
6. Grassing up disturbed senator is betrayal (7)
7. Goat can provide material for Roman cloak (4)
8. Equip badly to take offence (5)
9. Sadomasochistic film has long wait plus sick endings (6)
11. That is to say the laymen are confused (6)
15. Intelligent female support taken briefly to New York (6)
17. Inserted are components of one who lives there (8)
18. The sluices spewed an alternative to Fahrenheit (7)

DOWN

1. Being not warmed up before races leads to hilarious film about a Caribbean bobsleigh team (4, 8)
2. Bad dream about carrying a weapon (5)
3. Passed out defiant after riotous assembly (7)
4. Pressed beef gives you strength (5)
10. Warbled drunkenly and had a fight in a bar (7)
12. Shortly mother took the management graduate to see a venomous snake (5)
13. You can recreate amenity whenever you want (3, 4)
14. Deranged escorts provide sexy constraint (7)
16. The mnemonic making an ass of you and me is also known as that which makes one smile (6)

Hint: Anagrams are often indicated by 'confused', 'mixed up', 'components of', 'mistakes', 'deranged', 'mistaken', 'badly', 'wrongly', etc.

Circuit 3

Critics know the way but can't drive.

Kenneth Tynan

Q1 *We have adapted an old proverb for our new book on thinking. We have removed the vowels. What might the proverb be?*

   THNKTWCCTNC

Q2 *You dreamed a town hall was haunted. Who was there?*

Q3 *Use some or all of the operations indicated on the line to make each equation balance (=10). Use square brackets to embrace curved brackets.*

(A) Using no more than six 1s, $10 = (\ ) \times -$
(B) Using no more than six 2s, $10 = (\ ) \times \times +$
(C) Using no more than six 3s, $10 = (\ ) \times \times + \div$
(D) Using no more than six 6s, $10 = [\ ] (\ ) (\ ) \times + + - \div$
(E) Using no more than six 7s, $10 = [\ ] (\ ) (\ ) \times + + + \div$
(F) Using no more than six 8s, $10 = [\ ] (\ ) (\ ) \times + + + \div$
(G) Using no more than six 9s, $10 = (\ ) \times + \div$

Hint: For example, in line C, $10 = (3 \times 3 \times 3 + 3) \div 3$.

Clues: In line A, you can use two 1s to make 11.

Q4 *Pictured in a red bathing costume, her poster sold 8 million copies. Her* Cosmopolitan *cover in 1977 created a 'flick' hairstyle that was copied around the world. A prince polished her halo!*

   _ _ _ _ _ H / _ _ _ _ _ _ _ T (6, 7)

Hint: If you push it you might get her surname, but it will get you into hot water in Germany.

Q5 *Rather than quit and stay at the bottom, you could raise your*
word game

SPAR
_____

_____

_____

QUIT

Hint: Dress up for the barbecue and the rod that reaches across.

Q6 *Every block in this pyramid contains a number which is the sum of*
the two on which it rests. What are the missing numbers?

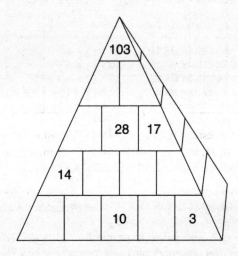

Q7 *Complete the Sudoku.*

1		3	5	4	6	7		
		7			8	2	3	
5	8				7		4	6
	1		3			8		7
		6				4	1	
			1		4		5	3
		1			2	9		
9				7	3		6	
		5	6	9	1	3	2	

On every circuit, questions 8, 9 and 10 will be about numbers – their significance in nature, mathematics, science, religion, mythology, art or history.

Q8 *Acting independently on* __ __ . __ __ . __ __ __ __ , *Thomas said that it was self-evident that all men were born equal and with the right to life, liberty and happiness.*

Hint: __ __ . __ __ . **1 7 7 6**

Q9 *19__ __ : Russia invaded Czechoslovakia and there were riotous student protests in Paris and Mexico City; anti-Vietnam War demonstrations in London; the assassination of Martin Luther King and Robert F. Kennedy in the USA.*

Hint: Life begins at __ __.

Q10 *'She was only __ __, only __ __. She was too young to fall in love, and I was too young to know' – so sang Sam Cooke. Singers from Chuck Berry to Julie Andrews have said how sweet it is to be this age. A double is the most popular checkout in darts and we are awake for this average number of hours a day.*

Hint: There are this number of chess pieces in a set, ounces in a pound and named points on a compass.

When you have worked out the titles of the next four films or TV shows, try to rent, buy or borrow and watch them. They are all brain workouts. They all involve emotional, visual and verbal thinking, plus either logic to aid your critical thinking or humour to aid your creativity.

Q11 *The post has come – sounds like you might have a partner.*

☐☐☐☐ ☐☐☐☐

Hint: What comes in the post that has the same sound as male?

Q12 *A medic we don't recognize was first shown on the day President J. F. Kennedy was assassinated.*

☐☐ ☐☐☐☐☐☐ ☐☐☐☐

Hint: Knock, knock. Who's there?

Q13 *If she was inside and went this colour before she went to hell she would need to be examined as she left.*

☐☐☐☐☐☐

Hint: If it is true that Eve was naked inside the garden, she might have been blue with cold.

Q14 *What do Roy Orbison and Richard Gere have in common?*

☐☐☐☐ ☐☐☐☐☐☐☐☐

Q15 *Which of A, B or C fits in the bottom corner?*

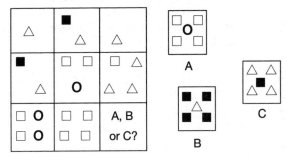

How did you get on?

Score 3 for each correct answer.

Score an extra 3 points if you did not use the Hints.

Enter your total here ☐

1 in 2 people can expect to score 10 or less when they start.

1 in 40 people can expect to improve their score to 70+.

Cryptic tip 3

As you may have realized by now, one of the most common ploys of the cryptic clue-setter is the anagram. We have already identified some of the common words that indicate that this is the cryptic operation required. Here is a fuller, but by no means exhaustive list:

abnormally	minced	restored
agitated	mislaid	revised
(all) at sea	misplaced	ruptured
all over the place	mixed	somehow
alterations	moved	sort
breaking (up)	out of	spoilt
camouflages	randomized	stormy
capsize	rearranged	strangely
changed	rebuilt	switched
chewed	recipe for	transfer
concocted	recovered from	troubled
conversion	redesign	(in) turmoil
converts	reformed	turned into
cooked up	re-laid	twisted
dealt	remade	unravel
disguised	remodelled	unusually
drunken	reordered	upset
erupts	rescheduled	variation of
extended	reshaped	wrongly
loosened	resorted	
manoeuvred	restoration	

If you suspect an anagram, check the number of letters required for the answer and look for a word in the clue with the same number.

For example:

▶ **Rene's** *upset is an INDICATION OF CONTEMPT* = *sneer*
▶ **Men test drive a** *convertible to obtain PROMOTION* = *advertisement*
▶ *Troubled* **masters sense** *NEED TO RESIT* = *reassessment*
▶ *MAINTENANCE OF POWER* **at mains** *exchange required* = *stamina*
▶ *PAINFUL SURGERY* **yet Dr isn't** *confused* = *dentistry*
▶ **Hat** *and* **pipe** *mislaid AT THE END* = *epitaph*

Cryptic crossword 3

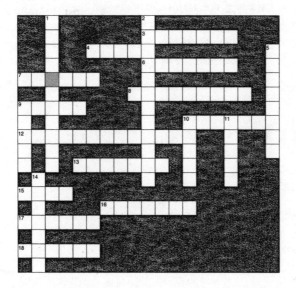

ACROSS

3. Hat and pipe both mislaid at the end (7)
4. Greek letter is mixed up with a note to a short mother (5)
6. Taken with mittens in which the last shall be first (7)
7. How could so confused a medic be so popular on TV? (2, 3)
8. Potentially painful surgery yet Dr isn't confused (9)
9. Rene's upset is an indication of contempt (5)
10. A gas Sue strangely cooked up turned out to be a common accompaniment of eggs (7)
12. Men test drive a convertible to obtain promotion (13)
13. Maintenance of power mains at exchange required (7)
15. Stand up at the Albert Hall was a romp (4)
16. In tears about the spoilt truffle (7)
17. The essence appeared in a tureen (6)
18. Billy Bunter's irritated retort to a bounder (6)

DOWN

1. Adam's partner was wrapped in azure velour to entitle this film (4, 6)

2. Troubled masters sense another test (12)
5. Capsizing cripples sailing ships (8)
9. Going backwards on trams can make you clever (5)
10. Dusty restoration of a place to write (5)
11. Spy on spoon in disguise (5)
14. Inventor rebuilt reactor (7)

Circuit 4

Before I learn to write legibly, I have to learn to spell correctly.

Terry Horne

Q1 *Fill in the two missing words so that the sentence makes sense. The two words you add should each have five letters and be anagrams of one another.*

He climbed _ _ _ _ _ , from which vantage point he hoped better to see the route along which he hoped his raft would _ _ _ _ _ .

Q2 *How would you be able to tell whether a three-eared person was known as Captain Kirk?*

Q3 *Create a set of letters corresponding to the set of numbers given. Rearrange the letters to give a word that relates (crossword style) to the clue given. The numbers represent letters according to their position in the alphabet, i.e. 1 = A, 2 = B, C = 3 ... Z = 26.*

(A) 20, 9, 18, 5, 19	**One never tires of going through their passage**
(B) 18, 5, 19, 5, 20	**One can reset the text so as not to waste words**
(C) 12, 1, 19, 20, 5, 4	**It lasted well when preserved in this way**
(D) 14, 5, 1, 18, 9, 20	**If you ever get near it you will not forget it**
(E) 12, 1, 19, 20, 20, 5, 5	**If you mess up the last tee, you will be sleepless there**

Q4 *Well known for her dramatic husky voice, she played the lead in* The Thorn Birds. *A* Cosmopolitan *cover girl in 1977. Continues as a successful film director, writer and fundraiser.*

R _ _ _ _ L / _ _ _ _ (6, 4)

Hint: Her first name hides her pain. Her surname would be useful in an emergency. Dr Stephen knew Christine, who led to John's downfall.

Q5 *Cute as you are now you can rise to have many people with whom you are popular.*

?

_____

_____

_____

CUTE

Hint: Incisive, decisive, cool and able to store a lot to feed you for your gig in front of lots of people.

Q6 *Every block in this pyramid contains a number which is the sum of the two on which it rests. What are the missing numbers?*

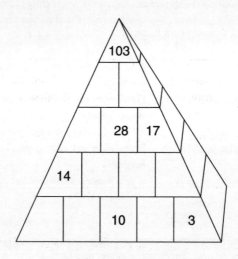

Q7 *Complete the Sudoku.*

1	2					6	9	
	5						3	
8	9		2	3			7	5
2	4		3		5	7		
	6		4			5	2	
		8			2	3		1
		2	7		9		5	
	3	4			1			
9		5				4	1	7

On every circuit, questions 8, 9 and 10 will be about numbers – their significance in nature, mathematics, science, religion, mythology, art or history.

Q8 *What do a salad dressing, a dome and a Roman mile have in common?*

__ __ __ __

Hint: The first number to be punctuated.

Q9 *The number of men on a dead man's chest. Andy Warhol said 'I'll be world famous for __ __ minutes.' Goethe said, 'Nobody looks even at a rainbow for more than __ __ minutes.' A cake from Northern Ireland that contains __ __ marshmallows and __ __ digestive biscuits. This century had a 100 years' war, Joan of Arc, the Spanish Inquisition, the Wars of the Roses, Beijing as the new capital of China, and the first condom!*

Hint: This square will magic the number to you.

8	1	6
3	5	7
4	9	2

Q10 ___ ___ is no longer a statutory retirement age in the UK, new life expectancies have changed all that.

Hint: This square can magic the number you need.

17	24	1	8	15
23	5	7	14	16
4	6	13	20	22
10	12	19	21	3
11	18	25	2	9

When you have worked out the titles of the next four films, try to rent, buy or borrow and watch them. They are all brain workouts. They all involve emotional, visual and verbal thinking, plus either logic to aid your critical thinking, or humour to aid your creativity.

Q11 *Should always be dark.*

☐ ☐ ☐ ☐ ☐ ☐ ☐ ☐

Hint: This is the French spelling because the film is set in France.
Should not be eaten dairy or white.

Q12 *Finally succumbed to the cold hard force of nature, despite the fact that a giant of a man was going to be in charge shortly.*

☐ ☐ ☐ ☐ ☐ ☐ ☐

Hint: Built by professionals, Kate appeared and Celine sang and the story goes on and on.

Q13 *Pirates eat in unaccompanied.*

☐ ☐ ☐ ☐   ☐ ☐ ☐ ☐ ☐

Hint: The only person in his house.

Q14 *Missile has a strong sense of identity.*

☐   ☐ ☐   ☐ ☐ ☐

Hint: Samuel mused 'I think, therefore...'.

Q15 *Which square fits in the pattern? A, B or C?*

Hint: Inside out or outside in?

How did you get on?

Score 3 for each correct answer.

Score an extra 3 points if you did not use the Hints.

Enter your total here ☐

1 in 2 people can expect to score 10 or less when they start.

1 in 40 people can expect to improve their score to 70+.

Cryptic tip 4

'To eat' can imply 'to go/put inside another word or phrase'.

For example:

▶ *Shortly* **Charles** *will get* **nothing** *to eat leading to* DISORDER *(5)*
▶ *Shortly/abbreviated Charles = Chas, gets nothing = O to eat = inside Chas = chaos (= disorder)*

The need to take out or extract letters, on the other hand, is commonly indicated by 'ex', or 'some', or 'some of'.

For example:

▶ *Ex-dragoons*
  Some dragoons ⎫ *laugh, telling of fierce attack (9)*
  Some of the dragoons ⎭
  *The answer is 'onslaught', that is: ex-drago**ons laugh, t**elling...*

'Belittle' is another way of indicating the need to abbreviate.
For example:

▶ **WE** *will belittle* **America** *shortly* = US

'Indefinite' indicates 'a' or 'an'. For example:

▶ *After an juniper drink an indefinite* PAIN IN THE CHEST
  So, after an + juniper drink + an indefinite = an + gin + a = angina = pain in the chest

A common way to get 'ab' at the beginning of an answer is to refer in some way to seamen – as in able-bodied (ab) seamen.

A common way, on the other hand, to get 'able' at the end of an answer word is to anagram 'Elba'.

Cryptic crossword 4

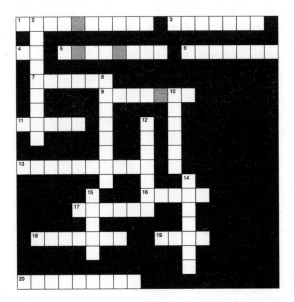

ACROSS

1. Pirates eat one meal unaccompanied in the house (4, 5)
3. Boat succumbed though giant of a man was going to be in charge shortly (7)
4. We will belittle America shortly (2)
5. Samuel asserted that a missile must first have a strong sense of identity (1, 2, 3)
6. Unravel threads – that's most difficult (7)
7. After an juniper drink an indefinite pain the chest (6)
9. An existential start stays down before rising to make enlarged film title (4, 2)
11. Little Charles will get nothing to eat, leading to disorder (5)
13. Summer on Elba somehow would be timely (10)
16. Three dissolve into sleepy air (5)
17. Danced and staggered after the blow (6)
18. Retrace cooked-up food supplier (7)
19. Eliminate words as the tide turns (4)
20. A carthorse moved a musical group (9)

DOWN

2. Some of the dragoons laugh telling of fierce attack (9)
8. Seamen before usual folk – that's odd (8)
10. Unions reorganize as with one voice (6)
12. The decreed alterations faded into the distance (7)
14. Alterations in density will determine our fate (7)
15. Oyster camouflages paler gem (5)

Circuit 5

The publishers of this book are to be congratulated on designing covers that are not too far apart.

Ambrose Bierce

Q1 Letters have been arranged around the edge of the two circular tables below. The same letter is missing from each table at the positions marked •. When you have inserted the correct missing letter you will be able to discover what your eastern guest is eating by walking around the tables.

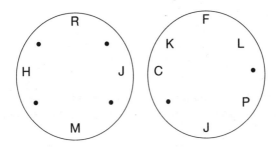

Q2 What would you call a space-travelling wizard?

Q3 Fill in the numbers in the bottom row.

3	3	6	9
15	24	39	63
102			

Hint: Numbers get longer from left to right, and progress similarly from one to the next.

Clue: Last number is > 400.

Q4 The poster of her as a sexy cave woman in a bikini is better known than the film from which it was taken – One Million Years BC (1966). Passionate about yoga, a Cosmopolitan cover girl in 1978, she is now a successful writer and business woman.

_ _ _ _ _ _ / _ _ _ _ _ (6, 5)

Hint: Sounds like artists suppressing the language of Wales.

Q5 You can rise from a dependent low life to make a go of things on your own.

_____?_____

_____

_____

_____

_____

VICE

Hint: Nasty at first you can make a lot by this kind of dancing, but you can better afford to ride horses once you can go it alone.

Q6 Every block in this pyramid contains a number which is the sum of the two on which it rests. What are the missing numbers?

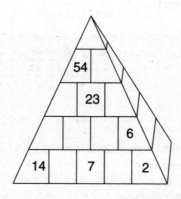

54

23

6

14   7   2

Q7 *Complete the Sudoku.*

	1	2			8	4	7	6
	4	7	1	2	6	5	8	
	6	8						
1		4	5	3		6	9	
6			8		1	2	4	
7	8	9	2		4	3		5
2					3	8		
4		1	7			9		2
		5	6	1				4

On every circuit, Questions 8, 9 and 10 will be about numbers – their significance in nature, mathematics, science, religion, mythology, art or history.

Q8 *Seven thousand years ago the Sumerians used the number _ _ _ _ to tell us by degree, where on earth we were!*

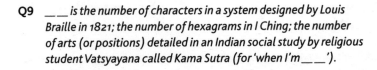

Hint: It is the smallest number that can be made by multiplying 24 other numbers together.

Q9 *_ _ is the number of characters in a system designed by Louis Braille in 1821; the number of hexagrams in I Ching; the number of arts (or positions) detailed in an Indian social study by religious student Vatsyayana called Kama Sutra (for 'when I'm _ _ ').*

Hint: The first number to be a square, a cube and sixth power.

Q10 *There are numerous references to _ _ rams, lambs, cubits and wives in the Bible, but in February this number is mostly associated with love and with the number of lines in Shakespeare's romantic sonnets, 'Shall I compare thee to a summer's day?'; Europe's longest-reigning monarch – the Sun*

King – reigned for 72 years from 1643, he was Louis __ __th of France.

Hint: There are thought to be this number of stopping places (stations) for Christ's cross on the Via Dolorosa.

When you have worked out the titles of the next four films, try to rent, buy or borrow and watch them. They are all brain workouts. They all involve emotional, visual and verbal thinking, plus either logic to aid your critical thinking or humour to aid your creativity.

Q11   *Tom Hanks goes for a rest and swallows gum before parking briefly.*

☐ ☐ ☐ ☐ ☐ ☐ ☐   ☐ ☐ ☐ ☐

Q12   *Definitely more than one article in France precedes mean person with abilities.*

☐ ☐ ☐ ☐ ☐ ☐ ☐ ☐ ☐ ☐ ☐ ☐ ☐

Hint: A musical with an unhappy French title.

Q13   *An existential start stays down before rising to make an explosive title.*

☐ ☐ ☐ ☐ ☐ ☐

Hint: A boxer's upper cut is inflated when photographs are enlarged in this way.

Q14   *Erin's surname becomes solid, shortly belonging, in a familiar way to Victoria Hospital, as foretold.*

☐ ☐ ☐ ☐ ☐ ☐ ☐ ☐ ☐ ☐

Hint: Try breaking up the surname __ / __ __ __ __ / __ / __ __ __ __ / __ – Julia Roberts battling against the capitalist powers behind a chemical plant.

Q15 *Which square fits in the pattern, A, B or C?*

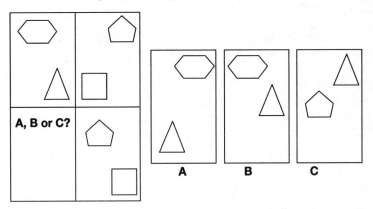

Hint: How did the pentagon and the square move?

Cryptic tip 5

Phrases along the lines of 'With North, South, East or West' indicate that the letters N, S, E and W will be used. Phrases along the lines of 'Without North, South, East or West' indicate that the letters N, S, E and W will not be used. (The word 'point', 'points' or 'pointer' may also be present.) For example:

▶ PEN POINTS *made about* **Ibsen** *not opposed by West (4)*
▶ *About Ibsen = anagram of Ibsen, not opposed by West = not East = without 'e' (remove 'e' from Ibsen) = nibs (4) = pen points*

For down clues, operations like 'climb', 'upside', 'upwards', 'up', 'ascending', etc. indicate that the reverse is required. For example:

▶ PLACE **to tie boat** *up (4, down)*
▶ *To tie boat up = moor, but 'up' in a down clue gives a reverse = room (4) = place*

Also look at:

▶ BODY BASED IN BELIEF is **prepared**, *including a* **cheer** *leader (4)*
  Cheer leader gives us a 'c' (lead letter of 'cheer') to include in 'prepared' – but we only have four letters, so prepared must be paraphrased to a three-letter word, e.g. 'set'. When we include 'c', we get 'sect' = a body based in belief (trying to insert 'body' into 'belief' would have needed many more letters than four!).
▶ BIG part of the **devastation** *(4)*
  *The number tells us that we are only looking for four letters, part of de*vast*ation = vast (4) = big*

Cryptic crossword 5

ACROSS

   3. Large part of the devastation (4)
   6. Tom Hanks leads search for remainder of the trees one gets stuck up before finding a place to park for a while (7, 4)
   7. Space to tie boat backwards (4)
   8. Pen points made about Ibsen not opposed by the West (4)
  10. Beheaded wizard found in German city (6)
  12. I blame Mario about things I remember (11)
  13. Repeated shouts of approval confused the district attorney briefly in a show of defiance (7)
  14. The backward doctor one knows is menacing (7)
  16. Broken wrist can lead to legal issues (5)
  17. Several broken cones are served with butter, jam and cream (6)

1. Existential start stays down before rising to explode as title for a film (4, 2)
2. Succeeding late in life (7, 2)
4. Neuroscience author is back before Monday (5)
5. Group prepared to include a cheerleader (4)
9. In October lingers a German city (6)
11. Giving out signals indicating time-up followed by a sound sensation (8)
15. The inexperienced intrude clumsily (7)

Circuit 6

We would like to thank Indexers, Society of, The

After Waterhouse, K.

Q1 *Every year, Simon takes children with Type 1 diabetes on an outward-bound holiday. This year he has organized a barbecue to raise funds. He goes to do the shopping and spends half his budget plus £10 on meat, half of the remainder plus £10 on sugar-free drinks, and half of what is then left plus £10 on fuel. He has £20 left. How much did he have in his budget to start with?*

Q2 *Abbreviated parent?*

M _ _ _ _ _ _

Q3 *Each of the following cards has a number on one side and a letter on the opposite side. Which of the following cards must you turn over in order to test a rule that 'if a card has a number one on one side, it has a letter A on its opposite side'?*

> **Hint: 2nd and 4th are not relevant to the rule being tested.** Need to check one card with the relevant number first.

Q4 *This Nicaraguan beauty was a snake fiend in* Never Say Never Again *(1983). A top model at 17, did she keep her famous promise to do nude scenes forever?*

_ _ _ _ _ _ _ A / _ _ _ _ R _ _ _ _ (7, 7)

Q5   Elevate your word skills so that you rise from the deck to be the captain.

<pre>
_____?_____

_____

_____

_____

_____
</pre>

DECK

Q6   Every block in this pyramid contains a number which is the sum of the two on which it rests. What are the missing numbers?

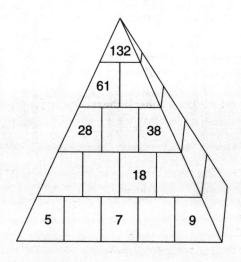

Q7   Complete the Sudoku.

	4		3	5				9
	6		1	2	9	7		5
	7	9	4	6	8	1	2	
2	1	3		8				
4	8		7		6	2	3	
6		7	2	1	3	4	5	
7		1		3				4
9	2		8		5			7
8		4						2

On every circuit, Questions 8, 9 and 10 will be about numbers – their significance in nature, mathematics, science, religion, mythology, art or history.

Q8   *For some, this number is the highly regarded product of two cubes, and the sum of three.*

Hint: The cube of the number is the result of multiplying the number by itself three times. E.g. 2 × 2 × 2 = 8; 3 × 3 × 3 = 27; 4 × 4 × 4 = 64; etc.

Q9   *Seven thousand years ago, the Sumerians devised a system of doing 'sums' based on __ __ which is still used in today's geometry and timekeeping, and the Chinese used this number of pegs in Chinese Chequers.*

Hint: The 19 __ __ s brought the pill, sex, drugs and rock and roll mixed with revolutions, assassinations and men on the moon.

Q10   *In the 1957 film ___ ___ Angry Men, Henry Fonda, playing number 8, started as the only one who didn't think the accused was guilty. It is the force of the strongest wind and the number of tribes who descended from Jacob.*

Hint: Jesus had this number of disciples and there are this number of days in Christmas and inches in a foot.

When you have worked out the titles of the next four films, try to rent, buy or borrow and watch them. They are all brain workouts. They all involve emotional, visual and verbal thinking, plus either logic to aid your critical thinking or humour to aid your creativity.

Q11   *The effect of the sun is fading in the final round of Come Dancing (in Paris).*

☐ ☐ ☐ ☐   ☐ ☐ ☐ ☐ ☐

Hint: The effect of the sun = tan and Marlon Brando's dance is from Latin America.

Q12   *When the Bard was In Love, it sounds like he made his weapon more intimidating, by waving it around.*

☐ ☐ ☐ ☐ ☐ ☐ ☐ ☐ ☐ ☐ ☐

Hint: This bard was born in Stratford, England, but his plays were performed at the Globe Theatre in London.

Q13   *Before you hear Miss Fitzgerald's first name, you will hear lots of bleating from both the drinking places you pass on the way.*

☐ ☐ ☐ ☐ ☐ ☐ ☐ ☐ ☐ ☐

Hint: In which Jane Fonda famously stripped under the effect of zero gravity.

Q14   *The top and bottom of it is you and I being helped to make another name for Mozart.*

☐ ☐ ☐ ☐ ☐ ☐ ☐

Q15 *The circumference of each of the identical pulleys A, B, C, D and E is twice the diameter of the axles to which they are fitted. If A turns at 200 cycles per second, at what speed will D rotate?*

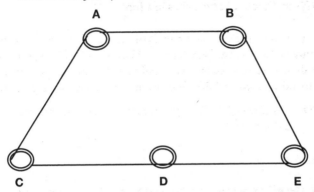

How did you get on?

Score 3 for each correct answer.

Score an extra 3 points if you did not use the Hints.

Enter your total here ☐

1 in 2 people can expect to score 10 or less when they start.

1 in 40 people can expect to improve their score to 70+.

Cryptic tip 6

Solve clues in numerical order, working across and down in parallel. This maximizes the number of crossovers. The resulting cross letters are all extra clues.

Look for the cross letter in the clues which cross. This helps to spot anagrams or part words or inserted words.

Present participles – words ending in the suffix 'ing' – are a gift. If the synonym in the clue ends in 'ing', the answer is also likely to. For example:

▶ **He** *has* **a ring** *for LISTENING IN COURT (7)*
   He + a + ring = hearing (7) = listening in court

Proper names often indicate an anagram. For example:

▶ **Stan gets a** *disguise IN STILL WATER (9)*
   Stan is probably part of an anagram of 9 letters, i.e. Stan gets a = stagnates (9) = in still water

Look out for double meanings, like 'Harry' = proper name and verb to attack or chase about. For example:

▶ *Harry the* **dragon** *with nothing to eat finds OLD STYLE SOLDIER (7)*
   Attacking the word 'dragon' and putting nothing, i.e. 'O', inside it yields dragoon (7) = old-style solider.

Cryptic crossword 6

ACROSS

1. Stan gets a disguise in still water (9)
3. The effect of the sun fading is what they are doing in Latin America, or latterly in a film shot in Paris (8)
5. He has a ring for listening in court (7)
7. Crafty afterthoughts about others keep him busy in the garden shed (7)
8. Harry the dragon with nothing to eat finds old-style soldier (7)
10. Bleatings from both holes lead to jazz start in film (10)
11. Sounds like a Welsh vegetable got crushed under the boat (4)
12. Tells a disturbed star female (6)
15. Barristers succeed in causing confusion about brute (5)
16. Snag is backward halfback (8)
17. The causes of the problem were revealed when torso was dissected (5)

DOWN

1. Rattle weapon to hear the Bard (11)
2. Goose flies out of danger (6)
4. Cross word weapon (5)
6. Film about Mozart indefinably made us (7)
9. Avid reversal reveals Prima Donna (4)
13. Gripping books after tea (6)
14. Herbaceous component of broken plate (5)

Circuit 7

In **Managing Public Services,** *I estimated that half of all senior managers were asses. I wish to withdraw my statement – half of all senior managers are not asses.*

After Benjamin Disraeli

Q1 *Fill in the missing consonants below and so clarify the word:*

E __ U __ I __ A __ E

Q2 *A joint of baby goat?*

K __ __ __ __ __

Q3 *Put a single digit in each box such that the sum of the digits = the total given in the clue for that row or column. Do not use any digit more than once for the answer to a given clue. Do not use zero. All clue answers end in an odd number (based on 'Adlock' by Gamon and Bragon www.brainwaves.com).*

Hint: Work in from the corners.

Clue: 10 down is 46829.

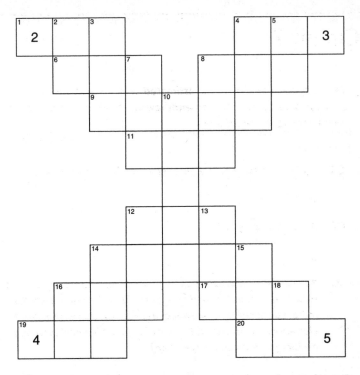

Across Total
1. 7
4. 8
6. 11
8. 22
9. 25
11. 22
12. 17
14. 34
16. 19
17. 20
19. 20
20. 17

Down Total
2. 6
3. 10
4. 13
5. 13
7. 18
8. 20
10. 29
12. 23
13. 18
14. 19
15. 24
16. 11
18. 12

Q4 *Chronically shy as a child, she eventually won a Golden Globe for LA Confidential in 1997. Recently voted the sexiest woman ever by Empire readers, she first appeared on the cover of Cosmopolitan in 1978 and is now president of PETA.*

__ __ __ / __ __ __ __ __ __ __ __ (3, 8)

Hint: Surname sounds more appropriate to a pub musician, or a sheep sewing machine!

Q5 *Okay you sank to the bottom, but you can still float up again and learn to stay afloat.*

_____ ?
_____
_____
_____
_____
SANK

Hint: After you sank you found yourself on the beach and spoke about being on these, but you will take the cream once you learn to stay afloat.

Q6 *Use only the numbers given to fill the vacant squares so that every row, column and both of the diagonals each total 219.*

13, 15, 108, 43, 42, 20

21, 12, 20, 19, 48, 15

46, 17, 51, 23, 62, 43

78	59			
			69	
63			66	
	80			62

Q7 *Complete the Sudoku.*

1			2			8		9
6		9	1		8	2	3	4
			4	9	1			
	1		4	8				2
			5		7			8
8			6	1	2			
		5	7					
	6			3	5		2	7
4	7							3

On every circuit, Questions 8, 9 and 10 will be about numbers – their significance in nature, mathematics, science, religion, mythology, art or history.

Q8 *What number do a triangle, a Fahrenheit thermometer and the work of the Sumerians in 5,000 BCE have in common?* __ __ __

Hint: Music to the ears of dart players.

Q9 *The 18__ __ s saw Darwin's* The Origin of Species, *a war in Crimea and a mutiny in India. One hundred years later saw James Dean, Elvis, Marilyn Monroe, the Cold War, the Suez Crisis, a war in Korea, the jive, mods and rockers and the beehive.*

Hint: Moses received the Torah after wandering round for one day less than this.

Q10 *The last minute is the __ __ th hour, and the same hour of the same day of the same month marks the end of World War I, which claimed the lives of 20 million people. A US airline flight of this number flew into a building that looked like this number, on this day, in September 2001. In 1960, Frank Sinatra, Dean Martin and Sammy Davis Jr made Ocean's __ __ and there were __ __ members of the gang that planned to rob the three biggest casinos in Las Vegas. The film was remade with George Clooney, Brad Pitt and Julia Roberts.*

Hint: Neil Armstrong used *Apollo* __ __ to land on the moon in 1969. This triangle will magic the number you require:

2

3   5

6   1   4

When you have worked out the titles of the next four films, try to rent, buy or borrow and watch them. They are all brain workouts. They all involve emotional, visual and verbal thinking, plus either logic to aid your critical thinking or humour to aid your creativity.

Q11 *The tricolour trilogy by Krzysztof Kieślowski.*

Three Colours…

☐ ☐ ☐   ☐ ☐ ☐ ☐ ☐   ☐ ☐ ☐ ☐

Hint: Set in France, Poland and Switzerland under the French flag.

Q12 *The actors are on holiday, especially Tom Hanks.*

☐ ☐ ☐ ☐ ☐ ☐ ☐ ☐

Hint: Drop some stitches or throw some ropes or tempting flies before you see a route.

Q13 *Brando's paternal deity.*

Hint: **Between God and her there was some surplus.**

Q14 *Typically, Hitchcock had the shrink cut exactly in half.*

Hint: **A shrink could be a psychologist.**

Q15 *The seats A–H on this seesaw are spaced at equal intervals from the pivot. John weighs 60 kg and sits at E. Jane also weighs 60 kg and sits at B. Jill also weighs 60 kg. Where should Jill sit to balance the seesaw?*

A	B	C	D	E	F	G	H

Hint: **The turning moments on one side of the pivot must equal the turning moments on the other.**
Turning moment = weight × distance from pivot.

How did you get on?

Score 3 for each correct answer.

Score an extra 3 points if you did not use the Hints.

Enter your total here ☐

1 in 2 people can expect to score 10 or less when they start.

1 in 40 people can expect to improve their score to 70+.

Cryptic tip 7

A plural clue must have a plural answer, often giving you an 's' at the end. (But watch out for cunning Latin plurals!) For example:

▶ *BLACKENED SAILORS of the* **Tsar** = *tars (anagram of 'Tsar' with 's' at end)*
▶ **Tsar's** *outstanding PERFORMERS = stars (anagram of Tsar's with 's' at end)*

He (or she) often indicates a profession, or a person doing something, and so the answer might well end in '-er'. For example:

▶ *HE PICKS THINGS UP MECHANICALLY scaring* **the long-legged birds** *(5, 6)*
 This is 'crane driver' (5, 6 ending in '-er'), i.e. he who picks things up mechanically and scares long-legged birds (cranes)

The use of '-ly' or '-lly' as a suffix in the synocript often indicates that '-ly' or '-lly' will be the last letters of the answer also. For example:

▶ *GENERALLY there is* **Public Land** *plus either end of* **Lindley** *(8)*
 *'Generally' means we are seeking a synonym ending in '-ly' (as found at either end of L*indle*y). Common (public land) + ly = commonly (8) = generally*

If you have a genre or category of things then you may be seeking a specific example of that generic category as your answer. For example:

▶ *'Beech' is a specific type of the generic category 'trees'*
▶ *'Ling' is a specific type of 'heathers' or 'fish'*
▶ *CASUAL WORKERS pay rent and still end up at* **Heather's** *(9) = hirelings*
▶ *KEEPING UP COURAGE in the dark after* **game of cards** *with* **Heather** *(9)*
 Game of cards = whist + ling (heather) = whistling (9) = (in the dark) to keep up courage

Cryptic crossword 7

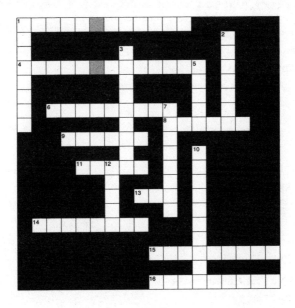

ACROSS

1. He picks things up mechanically shooing the long-legged flies further away (5, 6)
4. Kieślowski's tricolour number before we seize the pass (5, 7)
6. Commonly there is a senior military man at either end of Lindley (9)
8. An alcoholic drink indefinitely does not sound like heart disease (6)
9. Hitchcock cuts shrink in half (6)
11. Tsar's outstanding performers (5)
13. Sting by hustling NCO (3)
14. Referred to a ship's haven in a mouthpiece grown in water (8)
15. Casual workers pay rent and still end up at Heather's (9)
16. Keeping spirits up in the dark after game of cards with Heather (9)

1. Actors absent, especially Tom Hanks (8)
2. Can I raise a little tax for a Roman Catholic state? (7)
3. Brando's paternal deity (9)
5. Steaming fish was David's weapon
7. Young captain gives brief account of a stormy night sailing (8)
10. Chippies comes in after fish (10)
12. Someone from Scotland is royal place for punters (4)

Circuit 8

It was a clash between the will of the workers and the won't of the management.

Adapted from *Yes, Prime Minister*

Q1 *Please supply the missing number:*

10	12	44
6	14	40
4	6	20
14	12	?

Q2 *Is father's function a sell out?*

P _ _ _ _ _

Q3 *Bill owns 4 working suits – 2 black, 2 blue – and 3 pairs of dark burgundy leather shoes that each go well with each of his suits. He wears his suits and shoes in strict rotation every day of the week so that they 'recover' well in between. Perhaps because he always looks the part, he has been promoted again and celebrates by buying a new grey silk suit and a new pair of Bally shoes – again burgundy in colour. He wore his new combination today, 1 November. If he continues his former practice, on what date will he next wear his new combination of grey suit and Bally shoes?*

Q4 *She fronted a New Wave band named after her, belting out hits like 'Heart of Glass' and 'Denis'. A Cosmopolitan cover girl in 1978, she recently reformed her 1970s band and has an ongoing career as a jazz vocalist.*

_ _ _ _ _ _ / _ _ _ _ _ (6, 5)

Hint: At first the tide ran out between her spotted cubes and then her soiled surname launched a series of successful films for Clint Eastwood.

Q5 *At the moment you are only at the foot of the ladder, but if you can get yourself up a few rungs, someone can give you one of these.*

$$?$$

_____

_____

_____

_____

FOOT

Hint: The source of all is to be caring and to get close to others, in a group, so that someone can then give this you.

Q6 *Use the numbers given to fill the vacant squares so that each row and column totals 236. You may use any number more than once.*

4, 12, 14, 8, 25, 30, 31, 38

43, 46, 47, 51, 54, 59, 62

63, 66, 69, 74, 81, 130

	43		51	
	47		47	

Q7 *Complete the Sudoku.*

1	2	4	5	6	7	9	8	3
3	5	7	1	9	8	2	4	6
6	8	9	2	4	3	5	7	1
2	1	6	3	7	4	8	5	9
4	3	5	8	1	9	6	2	7
7	9	8	6	2	5	3	1	4
8	4	3	9	5	1	7	6	2
9	6	1	7	8	2	4	3	5
5	7	2	4	3	6	1	9	8

On every circuit, Questions 8, 9 and 10 will be about numbers – their significance in nature, mathematics, science, religion, mythology, art or history.

Q8 *This number – _ _ _ _ – was first scored on TV by snooker player Cliff Thornton. He started in 1983 but it was nearly 1984 by the time he finished! In 1997, Ronnie 'The Rocket' O'Sullivan achieved the same score in 5 minutes, 20 seconds.*

Hint: 15 × red, 15 × black, plus the 6 colours.

Q9 *After 7,500,000 years, Douglas Adams's Deep Thought worked out that the secret of life, the universe and all that was _ _, and the Egyptian god Osiris ordered that those who died would then be tried by this number of judges. The first book ever published, the Gutenberg Bible, has this number of lines per page.*

Hint: On 30 January 1969, the Beatles' last public performance –
impromptu from the roof of the Apple Studio in London – lasted
for this number of minutes.

Q10 *Possession is __ parts of the law, and you can be dressed to these
numbers and punished by a cat with this many tails.*

Hint: The digits of all multiples of this number always add up to
this number (or to a multiple of it). Also, if you invert any 3-digit
number and subtract the smaller from the larger, the middle digit
will always be the one you are seeking now.

When you have worked out the titles of the next four films, try to
rent, buy or borrow and watch them. They are all brain workouts.
They all involve emotional, visual and verbal thinking, plus either
logic to aid your critical thinking, or humour to aid your creativity.

Q11 *French girl starts by being unclear about me and ends in deceit.*

☐ ☐ ☐ ☐ ☐ ☐

Hint: Unclear, indefinite = A, about = on either side of (ME) and it
ends in a three-letter word = deceiving.

Q12 *It begins with deception and ends with a charge, after a good
car chase.*

THE FRENCH

☐ ☐ ☐ ☐ ☐ ☐ ☐ ☐ ☐

Hint: Deception = CON; electrified chemistry = ions – lots of links.

Q13 *Definite start to the times of work that ends up belonging to us.*

☐ ☐ ☐   ☐ ☐ ☐ ☐ ☐

Hint: Definite start = THE (definite article), and ends with
belonging to us = OURS.

Q14 *Although not at all detached, the centre of the title seems separate, though the end sounds like it is seriously intended.*

☐ ☐ ☐   ☐ ☐ ☐ ☐ ☐ ☐ ☐ ☐ ☐

Hint: A place to live that's not detached at all, and 'ment' sounds like 'meant' (seriously intended).

Q15 *The seats A–F on the seesaw are equally spaced. There is a child at A (30 kg) and an adult at E (60 kg). Where must another child (30 kg) go to balance the seesaw?*

30 kg	B	C	D	60 kg	F

Hint: Calculate the turning moments.

How did you get on?

Score 3 for each correct answer.

Score an extra 3 points if you did not use the Hints.

Enter your total here ☐

1 in 2 people can expect to score 10 or less when they start.

1 in 40 people can expect to improve their score to 70+.

Cryptic tip 8

Reference to a country – e.g. France, or French, or Parisian, or 'à la', or Gallic, or cross channel, or tunnel, or François, or just F – could mean that the answer contains a word, words or bits of words of the language of the country to which reference has been made.
For example:

▶ *DESCEND from* **TGV** *(7)*
  TGV = from French train = detrain (7) = descend
▶ **Eric** *is clearly going wild about* **the French** *GIRL (6)*
  Eric going wild = anagram of Eric, about = on either side of, the French = la = Claire (6) = a girl (clearly!)
▶ **Exciting** *start with* **Rome five** *in a* **French street** *is A THEATRICAL SHOW (5)*
  Exciting is 'e', + V (Roman 5), in rue (French street) = revue (5) = a theatrical show
▶ **Referring to German conjunction** *and* **gin**-*based cocktail is SHOCKING (10)*
  Referring to = as to, + und (German conjunction 'and'), + ing (gin-based cocktail) = astounding (10) = shocking
▶ *TIMETABLE for short-term* **primary education** *in* **German school** *(8)*
  Short-term/abbreviated primary education (first letters) = ed, in Schule (German school) = schedule (8) = timetable
▶ **Spanish exclamation** *in a trance after tea requires PATIENCE (9)*
  Spanish exclamation = ole, in trance after T = tolerance (9) = patience

Cryptic crossword 8

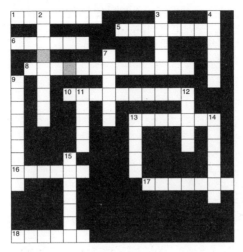

ACROSS

1. Descend from TGV (7)
5. Timetable for short-term primary education in German school (8)
6. She was filmed making an indefinite deception about me in France (6)
8. Film title was not detached though separate and seeming seriously intended in the end (3, 9)
10. Referring to German conjunction and gin-based cocktail is shocking (10)
13. Coastal area spreads disease (7)
16. Eric is clearly going wild about the French girl (6)
17. Fatherly sponsors play no parts (7)
18. Rapped more smartly dressed (6)

DOWN

2. Film has definite start to working times which begin with heavy breathing but which we own in the end (3, 5)
3. Exciting start with Rome five in French street opens show (5)
4. Remnants of past slicer unrecognizable (6)
7. The French water-ski on tropical lake (6)
9. Spanish exclamation in a trance after tea requires patience (9)

11. The geyser on the top can talk (5)
12. Sadness all round if Reg is upset (5)
13. Energetic mates can get up a head of this (5)
14. Energetic granny is winning (7)
15. Delicacy obtained after fretful search (7)

Circuit 9

Laws on the distribution of wealth ensure that shortages are equally divided among the peasants.

After John Graftson

Q1 *The value of dark chocolate:*

  6 bars of Mora Mora and 5 bars of Sambirano cost £36.00

  5 bars of Mora Mora and 6 bars of Sambirano cost £36.60

How much does each type of dark chocolate cost, per bar?

Q2 *Should you recycle this weapon?*

  S _ _ _ _ _ N

Q3 *Find word answers to the five clues and overlap them in the squares below; each starting on a numbered square part way through the preceding word.*

Clues

1 Something you sit at to eat (6)
4 Brain injury (6)
8 Bordering on New York (7)
14 Possess (3)
16 Brain cell (6)

1	2	3	4	5	6	7	8	9	10	11	12	13	14	15	16	17	18	19	20	21
T																				

Q4 *Born in Malibu, she was one of the all-time modelling greats for 20 years, until she crashed her helicopter. A Cosmopolitan cover girl in 1980, she is now a successful businesswoman.*

  _ _ _ _ _ _ _ _ / _ _ _ _ _ _ _ _ (8,8)

Hint: Christine's diminutive first name combined with 'edgy' second name.

Q5 *If a life of beer and sandwiches has made you feel low down the ladder, you can easily climb up to enjoy again flowing human kindness.*

_____ ? _____

_____

_____

_____

_____

_____ BEER _____

Hint: Sounds like sweeter route, can be driven but a higher toll charged, grates a lot but yields this flowing human kindness.

Q6 *Use the numbers given to fill the vacant squares so that every row, column and both of the diagonals each totals 190.*

6, 44, 40, 41, 42

24, 32, 33, 10, 16

29, 18, 47, 36, 38

38, 38, 13, 12

		52		59
	60			
	98			
				65
59				

Q7 *Complete the Sudoku.*

8				4		7		9
	1		7				2	
4			8					
				7		2	6	
7			6		9			4
	4	6		1				
					2			5
	9				1		7	
1		4		3				2

On every circuit, Questions 8, 9 and 10 will be about numbers – their significance in nature, mathematics, science, religion, mythology, art or history.

> **Q8** *A square dozen is a gross number – __ __ __ – which is important to players of* mah jong *and which you don't come across until the 12th position in a Fibonacci series.*

Hint: Found by degrees inside a decagon.

> **Q9** *As in WD __ __ and the number of days in Lent, its frequency in Muslim writings may be due to its Arab meaning of 'a lot'. After the American Civil War, General Sherman ordered that this number of acres be given to each freed slave.*

Hint: Ali Baba had this number of thieves.

Q10 *There are __ wonders in the world and you can sail that number of seas (many more actually). If you have a child until this age you will have created the person (Xavier, sixteenth-century missionary) who will go on to have this number of ages (As You Like It, Act II, Scene 3) – though Shakespeare's view is now outdated by neuroscience. The Austin __, Lotus __, and Caterham __ were popular British cars.*

Hint: Britain, Portugal, Prussia and Hanover took on the might of France, Russia, Sweden, Saxony and Spain in the __ Years' War between 1756 and 1763.

When you have worked out the titles of the next four films, try to rent, buy or borrow and watch them. They are all brain workouts. They all involve emotional, visual and verbal thinking, plus either logic to aid your critical thinking, or humour to aid your creativity.

Q11 *A mobile army surgical hospital in Korea shortly becomes the unlikely title of a smash hit comedy.*

☐ ☐ ☐ ☐

Hint: A way of eating potatoes that is popular in the UK with bangers (sausages).

Q12 *These Buddhists lived between what sounds like a large town and a sugar plantation.*

☐ ☐ ☐ ☐ ☐ ☐ ☐ ☐ ☐ ☐ ☐ ☐

Hint: A large town could sound like 'city' and a sugar plantation could sound like 'cane' and these kinds of Buddhist come between.

Q13 *The entrance to this large house is like the first word of Santa Claus's favourite triple word. You then pass many bedrooms like a hospital before you reach the extremity.*

☐ ☐ ☐ ☐ ☐ ☐ ☐ ☐ ☐ ☐

Hint: An extremity is an 'end'.

Q14 *The article and the Latin year end, contain a constant lot of keys to playing quietly.*

□ □ □   □ □ □ □ □

Hint: The keys, or ivories, can be black or white and need to be damped by pedals to produce the effect the name implies.

Q15 *Which square, A, B or C, fits best?*

A, B or C?

A

B

C

Hint: Imagine a mirror along each diagonal.

How did you get on?

Score 3 for each correct answer.

Score an extra 3 points if you did not use the Hints.

Enter your total here ☐

1 in 2 people can expect to score 10 or less when they start.

1 in 40 people can expect to improve their score to 70+.

Cryptic tip 9

When answers involve words from a modern European language it is usually signalled by including a reference to the country (see the Cryptic Tip in Circuit 8). No such reference is usually available when Latin words are used. These commonly include pro = for; re = about or related to; m or mille = thousands; am or ante meridian = before midday or morning; ditto or do = same again; Regina or Rex = queen or king or monarch; ult or ultimo = last; opus = a work; ante = before; ad = to, towards; vide = to see, as seen. For example:

▶ *ONE MANDATED TO VOTE* **for 2 algebraic variables** *(5)*
  Pro (Latin 'for') + XY (2 algebraic variables) = proxy (5) = one mandated to vote

▶ *SAVIOUR* **about** *to* **curse** *erratically (7)*
  Re (Latin 'about') + scuer (erratic anagram of curse) = rescuer (7) = saviour

▶ **Heavy soil** *contains* **thousands** *and is HOT AND STICKY (6)*
  Heavy soil = clay, containing thousands = containing Latin Ms = cla + m + m + y = clammy (6) = hot and sticky

▶ **In the morning** *sort of* **corny** *WORD FORMED FROM INITIAL LETTERS (7)*
  In the morning = between 'a' and 'm' (am = Latin 'morning'), sort of = anagram of corny = crony = acronym (7) = word formed from initials

▶ *Judge gave* **CD** *to* **monarch** *(8) = record to ER = recorder (8)*

Cryptic crossword 9

ACROSS

1. TTT is a teasing dance in South America (3, 3, 3)
4. Filmed instrument has mathematical value and plays quietly until the year end (3, 5)
6. One mandated to vote for two unknowns (5)
7. Punt almost disappeared with the wrong load (7)
10. There was a young rhyme in part of Ireland (8)
11. Ground for potters contains thousands and is hot and sticky (6)
12. A film initially entitled mobile army surgical hospital (4)
15. Firefighter about to curse short monarch improperly (7)
16. Applauds the increases even though they all start with a penny (7)
17. Dismiss the military paymaster (7)

DOWN

1. Buddhists live between what sound like a large town and a sugar plantation (7, 4)
2. French friends of English writer (4)

3. Howard met his demise in cinema (7, 3)
5. No man is not initially an island in this part of the Middle East (4)
8. Manual transport that prioritizes a familiar Richard before a British philosopher (8)
9. Initial word is corny in the morning (7)
11. Character from Greece caught despite sounding guilty is very smart (4)
13. Folds wind-blown petals (6)
14. Judge gave the tapes to the British monarch (8)

Circuit 10

I am a self-made man who worships his creator.

After Benjamin Disraeli

Q1 *Jog up a narrow road, leading to less fat.*

— — — —

Q2 *A sick-sounding symbol of the United States:*

I __ __ __ __ __

Q3 *Which is the most synonymous saying to: 'There's no such thing as a free lunch'?*

(A) All things come to he who waits.
(B) Where there's bees, there's honey.
(C) The only free cheese is in mousetraps.
(D) Too many cooks spoil the broth.
(E) The early birds eat the worms.

Q4 *A cover girl for* Cosmopolitan *in 1981, she has since appeared in* Not the Nine O'Clock News, *completed a PhD and married a famous Scottish comedian and actor.*

— — — — — — / — — — — — — — — — — (6, 10)

Hint: Shares a first name with Baywatch's best-known babe and a surname with the railway's best-known inventor.

Q5 *A toad is often at the bottom of the social ladder, but after only six steps, with one final bound you can be just one kiss away from royalty.*

?
_____
_____
_____
_____
_____
_____

TOAD

Hint: Urge happily that clothing and earthy footwear be sold off before one final bound.

Q6 *Use the numbers given to fill the vacant squares so that every row, column and both of the diagonals each totals 142.*

44, 24, 23, 36

30, 18, 8, 37, 22

48, 26, 19

		28		22
			28	39
25	32			
25			28	
	30	32		

Q7 *Complete the Sudoku.*

1	2					6	9	8
	4			6				3
6		8		3			4	
2		5		9	6	4		7
3		6	7					
4						3	6	1
		2	8			9	1	
		1			3			4
9	5	4	6	7		8		

On every circuit, Questions 8, 9 and 10 will be about numbers – their significance in nature, mathematics, science, religion, mythology, art or history.

Q8 _ _ _ *is the product of two numbers held in a sacred light. Perhaps that is why there is this number of beads on a Buddhist rosary, this number of girls enamoured of Krishna and this number of seats in the Parliament of Nepal.*

Hint: You can count up to this number in the Pentagon, even if they do not believe that 12 and 9 are sacred.

Q9 *The Anglican Church has _ _ articles and the old Wembley Stadium had this number of steps up from the pitch to the Royal Box – the title also of a gripping spy novel by John Buchan, made into a film by Alfred Hitchcock in 1935, remade in 1959 and 1978. Jack Benny celebrated this birthday 41 times before he died ('Age is mind over matter – if you don't mind, it don't matter!').*

Q10 *Punishment was __ of the best but the Birmingham __ were wrongly convicted. The numbers of wives of Henry VIII; the last word of the title of a book of children's poems by A. A. Milne (Now we are __); the number of types of 'quark' – one of three fundamental particles of which the universe is composed; the number of legs of the earth's most numerous species; strings on a guitar; points for a touchdown; points for potting a pink; protons in carbon atoms of which all life is composed.*

Hint: The smallest perfect number, it is the only number that is both the sum and the product of its factors. Take coins of any size and arrange them around one at the centre, so that the surrounding coins are touching. The number of surrounding coins will always be the number you are now seeking.

When you have worked out the titles of the next four films, try to rent, buy or borrow and watch them. They are all brain workouts. They all involve emotional, visual and verbal thinking, plus either logic to aid your critical thinking, or humour to aid your creativity.

Q11 *In this Italian film, sweet Italian girls spend their time between a young boy and a lively foam mattress.*

☐☐ ☐☐☐☐☐ ☐☐☐☐

Hint: French feminine singular *la*; the Italian for sweet is *dolce*; a lively foam mattress is Vitafoam.

Q12 *She is taught unclean movement to music.*

☐☐☐☐☐☐ ☐☐☐☐☐☐

Hint: What is the opposite of clean?

Q13 *The unclean lot from a baker's are offered freedom in return for a dangerous deed.*

☐☐☐ . ☐☐☐☐☐ ☐☐☐☐☐

Hint: For unclean see Q12. The final word finds small imperial measures hidden in their den.

Q14 *William the policeman starts by holding in a shout until I end up briefly over the top.*

☐ ☐ ☐ ☐ ☐   ☐ ☐ ☐ ☐ ☐ ☐

Hint: The boy dancer finally makes it from Tyneside to Covent Garden but the Oscar should have gone to Dad as well as Julie Walters.

Q15 *Which pane is likely to be smashed next?*

				*					A	B
	*								C	D
			*						E	F
			*						G	H

Hint: The vandals are moving clockwise in predictably increasing steps.

How did you get on?

Score 3 for each correct answer.

Score an extra 3 points if you did not use the Hints.

Enter your total here ☐

1 in 2 people can expect to score 10 or less when they start.

1 in 40 people can expect to improve their score to 70+.

Cryptic tip 10

Opus is the Latin word for 'work' (abbreviated to 'op' or 'ops').
One's magnum opus is one's great work. For example:

▶ **He** *accepts what* **little work** *there is in* THE BELIEF THAT
  THINGS WILL IMPROVE *(4)*
  *Op = little work, is accepted by He = hope (4) = the belief that
  things will improve*
▶ *Nothing works! (4)*
  O (nothing) + ops = oops!
▶ *EXPLOIT WORKERS* **working** *on a* **press** *(7)*
  op + press = oppress (7)
▶ *BETAMAX* **sees nothing** *(5)*
  Vide (Latin 'sees') + O (nothing) = video (5) = betamax

Numbers often indicate their Roman letter equivalents: 1 = I, 3 = III,
5 = V, 10 = X, 50 = L, 100 = C, 500 = D, 1,000 = M. A bar over the
top indicates thousands. For example:

▶ **Second-class one** *plus different* **sort** *makes special* CAFÉ *(6)*
  *Second-class = B + I (one) + stro (anagram of 'sort') = bistro (6)
  = café*
▶ *OLD FILES show that overarching* **search** *was arranged around*
  four *(8)*
  Four = IV, arranging 'search' around IV = archives (8) = old files
▶ **UNPICK** **French one** *and find* **quintet** *in* **real** *confusion (7)*
  *French one = un, + quintet = V, in anagram of 'real' = unravel
  (7) = unpick*
▶ **Six for each** *SNAKE (5)*
  VI (six) + per (Latin 'for each') = viper (5) = snake
▶ *At* **five** *to* **nine go back** *to the* **North East** *to find* MATERNAL
  FOX *(5)*
  *V (five) + IX (nine) + EN (North East backwards) = VIXEN =
  female fox*
▶ **None** *out of* **ten** *for spotting these* GIANT BEASTS **back in the
  North East** *(4)*
  *O (none) + X (ten) + EN (back in North East) = oxen (4) = giant
  beasts*
▶ *HIRED CARS* **thankfully** *turned up* **at eleven** *(5)*

*Ta = thankfully (or turn up 'at' = ta) + XI (eleven) = taxis
(5) = hired cars*

▶ *RESIDENT OF VILLAGE has **drink** after **6:50** (6)
Lager (drink), after VIL (6 + 50) = villager (8) = resident of
village*

Cryptic crossword 10

ACROSS

1. Second-class one plus different sort produces special café (6)
3. Resists work camera shots (7)
9. Betamax sees nothing (5)
10. Film shows the unclean imperial measures in the den (3, 5, 5)
11. Stellar film's opening hisses at the sailor and goes into battles (4, 4)

DOWN

1. Police yell and I go over the top on film (5, 6)
2. My mistakes! (4)
4. Film about recycling books (4, 7)
5. Unpick Parisian one and find quintet in real confusion (7)

6. Sounds like cannibal was pleased to have her on the menu for this film (9)
7. George Bernard is into flesh but redeems himself in great film part (9)
8. Go and overdose briefly on the northern hill as filmed (10)

Circuit 11

Minds are brilliant unless they are made up.

After Helena Bonham Carter

Q1 *Fill in the missing letters to find the basis of religion:*

_ _ E O _ O _ Y

Q2 *A parrot with its wings clipped?*

W _ _ _ _ _ / T _ _ _ _ _

Q3

108	356	496
196	780	292
284	648	?

Hint: Start by comparing (B – A) with C, remembering that as you come down the sign may change!

Q4 *The only one whose halo lasted five years of the show. First appearing as a cover girl in* Cosmopolitan *in 1981, she had a major success in* West Side Story *on Broadway and is now a writer of bestsellers, such as* The American Look.

_ _ _ L Y N / _ _ _ _ _ _ (6, 5)

Hint: Introduced in a positive German way to one who attaches good luck to horses.

Q5   *Stuck up a gum tree, or out on a limb, sounds like you can still reach upwards to find a couple of fruit and maybe some tasty game in the top branches.*

?
_____

_____

_____

_____

_____

TREE

Hint: Old fashioned and then plural pronouns in large numbers join together to rip these couplets of fruit from branches where game birds might be found on the first day of Christmas.

Q6   *Use the numbers given to fill the vacant squares so that every row, column and diagonal totals 118. You can use a number more than once.*

3, 27, 6, 24

21, 19, 8, 14

5, 23, 25

			21	43
	41	63		
27				37
	23	37		
39			50	

Q7 *Complete the Sudoku.*

		4	3			8	7	9
5			1	8	9	2	3	
9	3	8	2	4		1		6
	1			6		5	9	
6	4	5					8	
7				1	3			2
8	9			2	5	6	4	3
	7				1		2	
			6					8

On every circuit, Questions 8, 9 and 10 will be about numbers – their significance in nature, mathematics, science, religion, mythology, art or history.

Q8 *Signifying completion, _ _ _ is a milestone in sport and in top compilations. Its various names derive from the Greek* kekaton *the Roman* centum *and a Germanic word for a dog that can control about this number of sheep.*

Hint: The sum of the first: 4 cubes, 9 primes and 10 odd numbers.

Q9 *If you lay _ _ coins flat on a table you can make a hexagon. You then make a star by using 6 coins to create 6 equilateral triangles, one on each of the 6 sides. If you now remove the outer layer of coins, you will be left again with your original number of coins, but this time they will be in the shape of a six-pointed star – not the original hexagon! (Try drawing round a coin to investigate.)*

Hint: You have odds of __ __ to 1 against winning at Monte Carlo, where the roulette wheels start at 0 and go up to and including 36.

Q10   *It is the fifth number in the Fibonacci series; the number of planets visible to the naked eye; the number of Pillars of Islam and the number of minutes in a short break, as in 'take __ '.*

Hint: Genesis, Exodus, Leviticus, Deuteronomy and the Book of Numbers are the __ books of Judaism.

When you have worked out the titles of the next four films, try to rent, buy or borrow and watch them. They are all brain workouts. They all involve emotional, visual and verbal thinking, plus either logic to aid your critical thinking, or humour to aid your creativity.

Q11   *Not West is Not West.*

☐ ☐ ☐ ☐   ☐ ☐   ☐ ☐ ☐ ☐

Hint: Blocks from this direction in Europe have melted since the fall of the Berlin Wall.

Q12   *Also from an eastern culture, she wants to play football and Bend it...*

☐ ☐ ☐ ☐   ☐ ☐ ☐ ☐ ☐ ☐ ☐

Hint: Spicy marriage cooled it with Alex, so he moved to where it was really hot and then to LA.

Q13   *A medic of peculiar affection.*

☐ ☐   ☐ ☐ ☐ ☐ ☐ ☐ ☐ ☐ ☐ ☐ ☐

Hint: Medic = Dr and Peculiar = Strange.

Q14   *The first four letters definitely start things forward into art and all the food is finished in the end Mrs Robinson.*

☐ ☐ ☐   ☐ ☐ ☐ ☐ ☐ ☐ ☐ ☐

Q15 *What follows next, A, B or C?*

is to ... as ... is to A, B or C?

A   B   C

How did you get on?

Score 3 for each correct answer.

Score an extra 3 points if you did not use the Hints.

Enter your total here

1 in 2 people can expect to score 10 or less when they start.

1 in 40 people can expect to improve their score to 70+.

Cryptic tip 11

More on numbers:

▶ *SPITEFUL WOMAN stuck* **nine** *into beheaded* **diagram** *(5)*
  Diagram = Venn diagram, beheaded = VEN, insert IX =
  VIXEN = spiteful woman

▶ *After* **51** **were shouted at,** *they were FREE TO GO (9)*
  Fifty-one = LI + berated (shouted at) = liberated (9) = free to go

▶ *The SUBJECT today is the* **top 99** *(7)*
  Top + 99 = top + IC = topic (5) = subject

▶ *PUTS IN a thousand seedlings (8)*
  A thousand = IM + seedlings (plants) = implants (8) = puts in

▶ *Make deals with* **many farm workers** *(10)*
  Many = C (hundreds) + on tractors (farm workers) = contractors
  (11)

▶ *ANIMAL that's* **nothing** *like the sound of the one in* **the pub** *(4)*
  Nothing = O, in bar (the pub) = boar (4) = animal (The Boar =
  common pub name) (sounds like the pub bore!)

▶ *I was accepted by the* **men** *but after* **tea** *we found* **nothing** *outside*
  worth taking home as a SOUVENIR (7)
  I = me + men = memen + t = mement + O (nothing outside) =
  memento (7) = souvenir

▶ *DISCOVERED* **nothing** *in the* **fund** *(5)*
  O (nothing) + fund = found (5) = discovered

▶ *The French elected member with nothing on is OPEN TO*
  RIDICULE (7)
  The French = La + MP (elected member) + O (nothing) + on =
  lampoon (7) = ridicule

▶ *STARCHY PUDDING awaits familiar figure of* **Patrick**
  returning before **ten** *with his* **accountant** *(7)*
  Pat returning = tap + IO (ten) + ca (accountant abbrev) = tapioca
  (7) = starchy pudding

▶ **Indefinite number** *devour* **Scottish monster** *leaving NOTHING*
  OUT OF PLACE (8)
  Indefinite number = N + eat (devour) + ness (Scottish monster) =
  neatness (8) = nothing out of place

Cryptic crossword 11

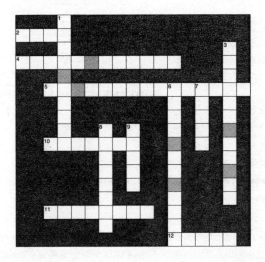

ACROSS

2. The brilliance of the first brother (not the other) is seen before 10 (4)
4. Dark chocolate digestives taken from nearer the back of the freighter (5, 6)
5. Secret French city is home of film (2, 12)
10. The queen goes after five and I go after tea fearing heights (7)
11. Subject of a film, start of which requires law briefly relevant to a negative chief executive in the Middle East (9)
12. The subject today is the top 99 (5)

DOWN

1. Filmed house had a number 51 (4, 5)
3. Musical film of the male magician of imperial weight (6, 2, 2)
6. 'Not west' is 'not west' reversed the film.
7. Hired cars thankfully turn up at eleven (5)
8. Resident of village has drink after 6:50 (8)
9. Discovered that there was nothing in the fund (5)

Circuit 12

Washington couldn't tell a lie.
Nixon couldn't tell the truth.
You need to tell the difference.

Terry Horne lecture notes, 2006, after Mort Sahl

Q1 *You can get a long way by filling in the missing letters:*

T R _ N _ _ O _ _ I _ E _ _ A L

Q2 *A frequent exclamation of juvenile indifference.*

W _ _ _ E _ _ _

Q3 *This crossword (based on Gamon and Bragdon www.brainwaves. com) has only 26 squares. You can use each letter of the alphabet once only.*

Hint: Write out the alphabet and cross out each letter as you use it. Near the end, try anagrams of the unused letters. Try starting with 5 across or 3 down.

Clues across

2. Vessel for punch
5. Wound
7. Anno Domini
9. Host
10. Sleeveless shirt

Clues down

1. Promise or 'the mess we're in'
3. Burdensome beast
4. Not real doctor
6. Short way
8. Turkish hat

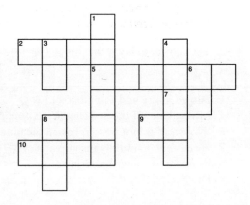

Q4 Daughter of Ingrid Bergman. After 14 years she was fired as no longer young enough to be the face of Lancôme. After appearing on the cover of Cosmopolitan *in 1983, and in* Blue Velvet *(1986), and* Fearless *(1993), she now, at age 55, markets her own cosmetics and skincare range.*

_ _ _ _ _ _ _ _ / _ _ _ _ _ _ _ _ _ _ (8, 10)

Hint: A short savings account becomes beautiful in Spain and then sounds like it comes in under sail.

Q5 *Start by reading those of others then word by word aspire to write one of your own.*

_____ ?

_____

_____

_____
READ

Hint: The way is measured in the old way, past the black bird, to your literary goal.

Q6 *Use the numbers given to fill the vacant squares so that every row, column and both of the diagonals each totals 111. You can use numbers more than once.*

3, 14, 20, 23, 6

22, 15, 13, 26,

17, 9, 38, 8

		28		26
	30	36		
	50		24	
29			22	
36				26

Q7 *Complete the Sudoku.*

		3	4	7		6		8
4		6	9					
7		9		6			5	
	1	4	8	3		7		
	6			5	2	4	8	
		8						
6		2				9		
	7		3	2	1	8	4	6
8	4		7		6			

On every circuit, Questions 8, 9 and 10 will be about numbers – their significance in nature, mathematics, science, religion, mythology, art or history.

Q8 *The right tangential number, __ __ is square and its decade saw more WWW, DVD, DNA, extreme sport, human cloning and global warming, and no more Soviet Union, East Germany, Czechoslovakia or Freddie Mercury.*

Hint: Thomas Edison patented hundreds of inventions, including the light bulb. Said creative thinking involved __ __ per cent perspiration and only 10 per cent inspiration.

Q9 *We have the Babylonians to thank for being able to combine __ __ with 7 in our daily lives. The Greeks used this number for their alphabet and Homer divided his Odyssey and Iliad into this number of books.*

Hint: This number of carats denotes gold in its purest form, i.e. 14 carats indicates a proportion of 14 parts gold to 10 parts other metals.

Q10 __ time is the most common rhythm in music, and there were __ Horsemen of the Apocalypse; __ cardinal points; __ seasons; __ Greek elements; __ apostles in Christianity; the __ Tops sang 'I'll Be There' in 1966; after Mao's death, his wife Jiang Qing, together with Zhang Chanqiao, Yao Wenyuan and Wang Hongwen were arrested as the Gang of __ who caused the Cultural Revolution of the 1960s.

Hint: __ letter word; __ poster bed; __ minute warning; __ suits of playing cards; __ movements in a classical symphony.

When you have worked out the titles of the next four films, try to rent, buy or borrow and watch them. They are all brain workouts. They all involve emotional, visual and verbal thinking, plus either logic to aid your critical thinking or humour to aid your creativity.

Q11 *Life is a taxi ending with tea, my friend.*

☐ ☐ ☐ ☐ ☐ ☐ ☐

Hint: A variety show at which you sit at tables.

Q12 *A cream cheesy state film in which lawyer Tom Hanks is discriminated against because he has AIDS.*

☐ ☐ ☐ ☐ ☐ ☐ ☐ ☐ ☐ ☐ ☐

Hint: Phil goes to find the Greek oracle but it ends indefinitely in a state in the USA.

Q13 *To put an end to being laughed at by a parrot, it is necessary.*

TO KILL A

☐ ☐ ☐ ☐ ☐ ☐ ☐ ☐ ☐ ☐ ☐

Q14 *Sounds like a male driver of a horse and carriage is needed during a severe drought.*

□□□□ □□□

Q15 *What's next, A, B or C?*

What's next?
A, B or C?

A   B   C

Hint: Try moving dots clockwise, maintaining the spacing.

Cryptic tip 12

Do not leap to numerical answers until you have first checked out if it's an anagram. If it's an anagram, the number is a red herring. For example:

▶ *One real messed up girl (7)*
▶ *This is an anagram of 'one real', so no need to be looking for 'I' in the answer = Eleanor (7) = girl*
▶ *Varieties of nine great fruit (9)*
  = tangerine (not a word with 9, ix)
▶ *About ten of the new trains were shortlived (9)*

Beware as there are two anagrams here. New trains = transi, + about ten = ent = transient (9) = shortlived

Sometimes the clue indicates that the answer contains a specific example of numbers:

▶ *Numerical alternatives to three voices (6)*
  Ten (numerical) + ors (alternatives) = tenors (6) (as in The Three Tenors)
▶ *Encourage as you listen to a song (7)*
  Listen = hear + song (is a number) = hear + ten = hearten (7) = encourage
▶ *A large number enquire about real beer (4)*
  Large number = C + ask (enquire) = cask (4) = real beer
▶ *Actual number in the region (5)*
  Actual = real + M (a number) = realm (5) = a region
▶ *Although a great number was included by the trio, they shook with nerves (7)*
  Trio = treble, including M (a great number) = tremble (7) = shook with nerves
▶ *We hear that a number had a meal (5)*
  = eight (5) (we hear 'ate')
▶ *Many hurried to the fruit (9)*
  Many = C + ran (hurried) + berry = cranberry (9) = fruit
▶ *Many make a row (6)*
  Many = M + align = malign (6) = row

Cryptic crossword 12

ACROSS

1. Southern fruit is a weapon (5)
4. Many hurried to the fruit (11)
6. A number had a meal, we hear (5)
7. A musical like a taxi by mistake before tea, my friend (7)
8. Fisherman starts by finding a corner (6)
10. One real messed up girl (7)
14. Supervision above vision (9)
15. Artist briefly in male film (4, 3)
16. American uncle leads bachelor a merry dance (5)
17. Sounds like removing the sign again will change the law (6)
18. Encourage as you listen to a song (7)
19. Numerical alternatives to three voices (6)

DOWN

2. A cheesy film state in which Phil finds an oracle before it ends indefinitely (12)
3. Many make a row (6)

5. Former writers I have found to be costly (9)
9. Accountant to steal poor substitute for dark chocolate (5)
11. Believed in canine mother briefly (5)
12. Of course aunt is in a mess before the race (9)
13. Variations of nine great fruit (9)
16. Reversing fruit layer produces the rest (5)

Circuit 13

My conversation has occasional flashes of delightful silence.

Simon Wootton, 2007

Q1 *It might take you a while to find the following five letters at this pace.*

The first letter is in stars and a seventh heaven,

The second is in none and also in eleven,

The third is in any and inside of play,

The fourth is in kind and also in weigh,

You'll find the fifth one hot, if from heaven you stray.

Q2 *Image makers used to come in suntanned cartons:*

B __ __ / B __ __ __ __ __ __

Q3 *Rearrange each of the following letter groups to form a word. Place the words in a 5 × 5 grid, vertically and horizontally.*

1. A E H S V
2. A E H N V
3. A E R T V
4. E E R S V
5. E E R N T

Hint: 1 = shave.

1	2	3	4	5
2				
3				
4				
5				

Clues

1. requires razor or plane
2. place of safety
3. avoid
4. poetry
5. sign of welcome

Q4 *Born in Australia and known as 'The Body', she became a 1980s supermodel. She appeared on the cover of* Cosmopolitan *in 1985. Now over 40, she is still modelling and is also a successful businesswoman.*

_ _ _ _ / _ _ _ _ _ _ _ _ _ _ (4, 10)

Hint: Lady in France goes to get unhealthy food for her male child.

Q5 *At the bottom you have only one coin, but a philosophical word at a time, you can turn it into something better proofed against inflation.*

?
_____

_____

_____

_____
COIN

Hint: Trade up for this staple and tie up with the next until the temperature drops, then exchange for that which glitters and belongs not to a fool.

Q6 *Use the numbers given to fill the vacant squares so that every row, column and both of the diagonals each totals 91. You can use a number more than once.*

4, 10, 9

23, 19, 18, 11

12, 17, 13

31				21
23				29
	38		22	
	24	27		
		21	21	

Q7 *Complete the Sudoku.*

	9		3	4	5	6	7	
		5	6		8			
6			1			3		5
5	3		4	8	6	1	9	
2			7		3	5		
							6	3
	2						5	
	6			1		8		
	5						2	

On every circuit, Questions 8, 9 and 10 will be about numbers – their significance in nature, mathematics, science, religion, mythology, art or history.

Q8   *With this number, _ _ , Abe so began a two-minute address dedicated to the proposition that 'All men are born equal'. The world will little note nor long remember what was said, but will not forgive what we do not do to complete the work of those who gave their lives to ensure that government of the people, by the people, for the people, shall never perish from this earth. 'Four score years and ten...'*

Hint: **Sum of the squares of the first four primes.**

Q9   *History says they stabbed Caesar _ _ times, but Shakespeare's Octavius added ten cuts for good measure in Act V, scene 1. The axis of the earth is so tipped and the Tropics move the same north and south of the equator. Worn by Michael Jordan in Chicago, Shane Warne in Australia and David Beckham in Madrid.*

Hint: **A favourite psalm at funerals.**

Q10   *'Now there are _ steps to heaven' according to Eddie Cochrane (1960) and that appears to be borne out by Christianity (Father, Son and Holy Spirit); Islam (Mecca, Medina, Jerusalem); Taoism (Yin, Yang and Man); Hinduism (Brahma, Shiva and Vishnu); Buddhism (Buddha, Dharma, Sangha).*

Hint: **_ little pigs; _ billy goats gruff; _ blind mice; _ wise men.**

When you have worked out the titles of the next four films, try to rent, buy or borrow and watch them. They are all brain workouts. They all involve emotional, visual and verbal thinking, plus either logic to aid your critical thinking, or humour to aid your creativity.

Q11   *The Austrian hills are alive with the...*

□ □ □ □ □ □   □ □ □   □ □ □ □ □ □

Hint: **Julie Andrews helps the Von Trapp family to climb every mountain to escape the Nazis.**

Q12 *Who hummed the Harry Lime theme? Not the first, not the second, but...*

□ □ □   □ □ □ □ □   □ □ □

Hint: Black-and-white grainy Cold War spy film is a bit of a *ménage à trois*.

Q13 *Was in the tale of two con men in the Wild West, memorable for the piano piece that is still one of the best-selling music sheets for piano.*

□ □ □   □ □ □ □ □

Hint: A risk around bees, wasps and scorpions – it's in the tail!

Q14 *Humphrey Bogart on a jungle river near Victoria Falls, the regal boat was called the...*

□ □ □ □ □ □ □   □ □ □ □ □

Hint: If Freddie Mercury's band had been out of Africa...

Q15 *Which of the following, A, B, C or D, can be folded into a complete cube without overlapping the faces?*

A   B   C   D

Hint: To achieve a full wrap around you must have a run of at least four faces.

How did you get on?

Score 3 for each correct answer.

Score an extra 3 points if you did not use the Hints.

Enter your total here ☐

1 in 2 people can expect to score 10 or less when they start.

1 in 40 people can expect to improve their score to 70+.

Cryptic tip 13

▶ Zero – zero has only been in Western mathematics for about 800 years. al-Khwārizmī, the Persian mathematician, had used it 400 years earlier, based on work by Indian mathematicians. It can turn up in cryptics as love (after the French for 'egg' – œuf), none, nothing, etc.

▶ One – can turn up as ace, once, unity, unitary or the letter i or I.

▶ Two – can turn up as deuce, twice, pair, twin, twain, duel or dual, couple, double, bi, binary, ii or II.

▶ Three – try, thrice, trio, triplets, trinity, iii or III. Or as fates, furies, graces, muses, denials, dimensions.

▶ Four – quartet, IV, elements, humours, cardinal points of the compass, quarters, corners of the world/earth, winds, rivers of paradise, or IIII on some clocks (Big Ben is wrong) and Einstein's dimensions.

▶ Five – quintet, quins, quintuplets, V.

▶ Six – half a dozen, sextet, sextuplets.

▶ Seven – septet, week, lucky.

▶ Eight – crew, octet, octane (as in notes in music).

▶ Ten – decimal, fingers, toes, X.

▶ Eleven – players, palindromic number.

▶ Twelve – months, signs (zodiac), hours, ides.

▶ Thirteen – unlucky, cards in a suit, baker's dozen.

▶ Fourteen – stone (14 lb), a fortnight.

▶ Fifteen – team, 15 red balls in snooker triangle.

▶ Twenty – a score.

▶ Twenty-four – hours.

▶ Twenty-eight – lunar month, dominoes in a set.

▶ Thirty-two – freezing point in degrees Fahrenheit.

▶ Thirty-seven – body temperature.

▶ Forty – long time, days in wilderness, rain, desert.

Cryptic crossword 13

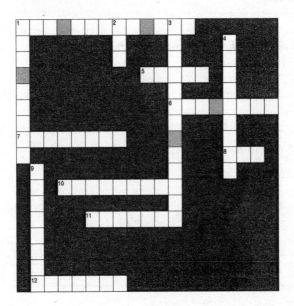

ACROSS

1. Film about the bronze medal male is one of a ménage (3, 5, 3)
5. Number one in the community (5)
6. The whole lot is covered and the fat lady sings (3, 4)
7. Insensitive start confused deer and made it difficult to get them counted (8)
8. Many left initially to go back (3)
10. Flexible relatives (9)
11. Confusing caution results in lots being knocked down (7)
12. Girl reversing can list a lot of dates (7)

DOWN

1. Film about the snake leader sounding like a bell (3, 5)
2. Line of argument (3)
3. Film about a Friday initially reorganized African National Conference and Freddie's band. (7, 5)
4. Sleeping plants a lot of short bullets a long way away (9)
9. Fill a lot randomly to launch a small fleet (8)

Circuit 14

Alas poor Yorick, I know him backwards.

Q1 *The same three letters will complete the following four words:*

_ _ _ E P, _ _ _ _ E N, _ _ _ _ L L, _ _ _ _ A T H

Q2 *It can produce a ceiling corner untouched:*

W _ _ S _ _ _

Q3 *Create a string of 24 letters containing overlapping words to which the numbered clues apply:*

1	2	3	4	5	6	7	8	9	10	11	12	13	14	15	16	17	18	19	20	21	22	23	24

Clues

1. French wine
3. New operational replacement stock
6. Confidence trick
8. Can't remember!
14. Reply
16. Short direction
17. A neuroscientist in a well-known area
20. A police verb (hopefully!)

Q4 *She appeared on the cover of* Cosmopolitan *in 1990. By 2001, she had won a Golden Globe for best actress and was also the most successful female songwriter of all time. Now in her 50s, three of her video recordings are banned as too sexy by MTV ('Justify', 'Erotica' and 'What It Feels Like for a Girl').*

_ _ _ _ _ _ _ (7)

Q5 Start at the bottom by finding somewhere to pitch your tent, then rise slowly by stages, until you need this for your new factory or office.

_____?_____

_____

_____

_____
CAMP

Q6 Use the numbers given to fill the vacant squares so that every row, column and both of the diagonals each totals 78.

15, 5, 3

16, 19, 4, 22, 11

14, 7, 13

23				17
	15		25	
		8	38	
33	15			
		24		27

Q7 *Complete the Sudoku.*

			6	5				
1	5							
	9	8	1					
	1		4		6		9	
	7	9	3			1		
4		6	5				2	
			9		3	4		5
	6	5		4	2			1
9	4						7	

On every circuit, Questions 8, 9 and 10 will be about numbers – their significance in nature, mathematics, science, religion, mythology, art or history.

Q8 *Pareto made a rule of it and Phileas too, __ __ days to do what Ellen did in 8 days fewer, what the US air force did in 94 hours (and 1 minute) in 1949 and what Australian Dave Kunst did on foot, in 1974, taking 1,568 days and 21 pairs of shoes.*

Hint: In the __ __ s, out went Iron Curtains, Berlin Walls, apartheid, LPs and hippies and in came solidarity, yuppies, PCs, CDs, crack, AIDS and mobile phones for keeping score.

Q9 *Joseph Heller's Yossarian was caught in this catch, along with players of American football and field hockey. __ __ yards in a chain, stops in an aperture and bones in a skull, it is a Frenchman's warning that the 'cops are coming'.*

Hint: Needed at one time to play soccer.

Q10 *Woody Allen said he felt at __ with nature. In old English, Mark __ never allowed school to interfere with his education.*

Hint: __ for one is a supermarket offer. These heads are better than one because they have company.

When you have worked out the titles of the next four films, try to rent, buy or borrow and watch them. They are all brain workouts. They all involve emotional, visual and verbal thinking, plus either logic to aid your critical thinking, or humour to aid your creativity.

Q11 *Clint Eastwood has never been pardoned, he remains...*

☐ ☐ ☐ ☐ ☐ ☐ ☐ ☐ ☐ ☐

Hint: No mercy shown in this classic Western.

Q12 *A great collie favourite gave his name to a brand of dog food.*

☐ ☐ ☐ ☐ ☐ ☐

Hint: Begins as a lady from Lancashire, that is.

Q13 *A short extraterrestrial wanted to go home.*

☐ ☐

Hint: 'Short', like 'brief' or 'contracted', often refers to the use of an abbreviation.

Q14 *In numerical incarnations, Simba, head of the jungle, was a favourite with kids and his songs went into the charts.*

☐ ☐ ☐   ☐ ☐ ☐ ☐   ☐ ☐ ☐ ☐

Hint: Sounds like this jungle monarch was not telling the truth – lyin 'sounds like'...

Q15 *What comes next, A, B or C?*

Hint: Count the number of sides in each column.

How does your score compare to Circuit 1?

Cryptic tip 14

'First' is usually telling you which parts of the clue refer to the start of the answer word. For example:

▶ *After first confusing alternative, it comes to be a cloak (4)*
  Alternative = or, confusing = ro + be = robe (4) = cloak
▶ *Freud had most luck first before getting his idea clear (5)*
  Most of luck first = luc + id (Freud's idea) = lucid (5) = clear
▶ *Thrifty girl first messed up her fur (6)*
  Starting with messed up fur = fru + gal (girl) = frugal (6) = thrifty
▶ *Try to tease at first (7)*
  At first = at + tempt (tease) = attempt (7) = try
▶ *To protect watch over vault first (9)*
  vault first = safe + guard (watch over) = safeguard (9) = protect

Examples of handy cryptic jargon:

▶ *Stay second (5) = support*
▶ *Fractional district (7) = quarter*
▶ *First person coins a lady (5) = penny*
▶ *Second eleven collapse (7) = subside (7)*
▶ *Went first round the snake and climbed the staking (8)*
  Went first = led; round the snake (adder) = laddered (8)
  = climbed up
▶ *Graduates before long gets first wind player (10)*
  Graduates = BAs + soon (before long) + ist (first) = bassoonist
  (10) = wind player
▶ *Being was first in French church (9)*
  Was = ex + ist (first) + en (French for 'in#) + ce (church)
  = existence (9) = being
▶ *Again allowed to rent (5)*
  Re (again) + P = relet (5) = rent again
▶ *Second-class one plus different sort of eating place (6)*
  Second-class = B + I (one) + anagram of sort = bistro (6)
  = eating place
▶ *Deleted record on other sort of unit ends up fifth rated (12)*
  Record = disc + on + unit (anagram – other sort of) + e (fifth
  rated) = discontinued (12) = deleted
▶ *Troubled masters sense second marking (12)*
  anagram of masters sense = reassessment (12) = second marking

Cryptic crossword 14

ACROSS

1. Sounds like this jungle monarch did not tell the truth in the film (3, 4, 4)
5. Film lacking mercy has different fun optionally donated (10)
8. Survival was first in French church (9)
11. Thrifty girl from the south first messed up her fur (6)
13. Try to tease at first (7)
14. First past the post coined a lady (5)
15. Graduates before long get first wind player (10)
17. Led round the snake it still ruined her stocking (8)

DOWN

2. The dog filmed in Los Angeles briefly has the secret service first before the fifth grade (6)
3. The first confused alternative came to be a cloak in the film (3, 4)
4. Mainly luck before getting Freud's idea clear (5)
6. Renting must be allowed again (5)
7. Troubled masters sense need for second marking (12)

9. Second eleven collapsed (7)
10. Neat prose translates into international language (9)
12. Four areas of town produce four half pints for the monarchs (8)
16. Second Corset (7)

Answers

Circuit 1

Q1   fear, pear, peas, peps, pops, hops, hope

Q2   When it's ground.

Q3   A = 2, B = 0, C = 4, D = 6, E = 1, F = 8, G = 7

Q4   Maud Adams

Q5   laze, daze, doze, done, dons

Q6

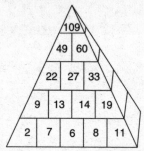

Q7

2	5	6	3	4	7	8	9	1
8	1	9	2	5	6	7	3	4
4	3	7	1	9	8	2	6	5
1	2	3	4	6	9	5	7	8
6	4	8	5	7	2	3	1	9
7	9	5	8	1	3	6	4	2
3	6	1	9	2	5	4	8	7
5	8	4	7	3	1	9	2	6
9	7	2	6	8	4	1	5	3

Q8 1,000,000
Q9 12
Q10 20
Q11 *Apollo (13)*
Q12 *Pay It Forward*
Q13 *The Pianist*
Q14 *Gandhi*
Q15 *A*

Cryptic crossword 1

Circuit 2

Q1

1	3	4	0	2
4	0	2	1	3
2	1	3	4	0
3	4	0	2	1
0	2	1	3	4

Q2 Use **a** spirit level!

Q3

6	6	12	18
30	48	78	126
204	330	534	864

Q4 Beverly Johnson

Q5 eggs, ergs, errs, ears, bars, bard

Q6

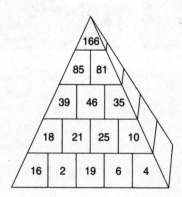

Q7

1	2	3	4	6	5	7	8	9
4	5	7	8	2	9	1	3	6
6	8	9	1	3	7	2	4	5
5	1	2	3	7	4	9	6	8
7	3	8	5	9	6	4	1	2
9	4	6	2	8	1	3	5	7
2	6	4	7	1	8	5	9	3
3	9	1	6	5	2	8	7	4
8	7	5	9	4	3	6	2	1

Q8 1984 (rework of '1948'; title of last novel by George Orwell)
Q9 69
Q10 19
Q11 *Dead Poets (Society)*
Q12 *On Golden Pond*
Q13 *Quills*
Q14 *Cool Runnings*
Q15 18

Cryptic crossword 2

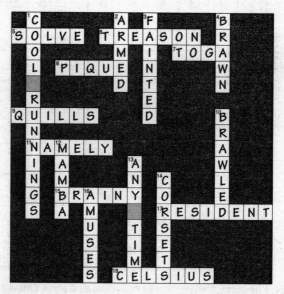

Circuit 3

Q1 Think Twice Cut Once
Q2 A night mayor?
Q3 Just check that the right-hand sides compute to 10.
Q4 Farrah Fawcett
Q5 quit, suit, spit, spat, spar

Q6

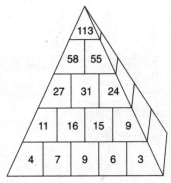

Q7

1	2	3	5	4	6	7	8	9
4	6	7	9	1	8	2	3	5
5	8	9	2	3	7	1	4	6
2	1	4	3	6	5	8	9	7
3	5	6	7	8	9	4	1	2
7	9	8	1	2	4	6	5	3
6	3	1	4	5	2	9	7	8
9	4	2	8	7	3	5	6	1
8	7	5	6	9	1	3	2	4

Q8 04.07.1776
Q9 68
Q10 16
Q11 *You've Got Mail*
Q12 *Dr Who*
Q13 *Blue Velvet*
Q14 *Pretty Woman*
Q15 C

Cryptic crossword 3

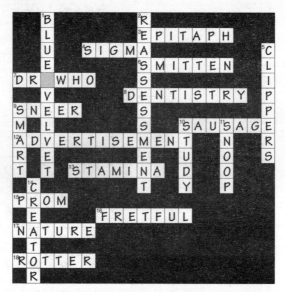

Circuit 4

Q1 aloft, float

Q2 If he had a left ear, a right ear and a final front ear.

Q3 (A) TIRES becomes RITES
(B) RESET becomes TERSE
(C) LASTED becomes SALTED
(D) NEAR IT becomes RETAIN
(E) LAST TEE becomes SEATTLE

Q4 Rachel Ward

Q5 cute, cuts, cats, cans, fans

Q6

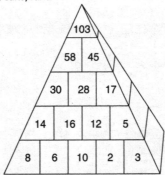

Q7

1	2	3	5	7	8	6	9	4
4	5	7	1	9	6	2	3	8
8	9	6	2	3	4	1	7	5
2	4	9	3	1	5	7	8	6
3	6	1	4	8	7	5	2	9
5	7	8	9	6	2	3	4	1
6	1	2	7	4	9	8	5	3
7	3	4	8	5	1	9	6	2
9	8	5	6	2	3	4	1	7

Q8 1,000 (Thousand Island dressing, Millennium Dome, Roman mile = 1,000 paces)

Q9 15

Q10 65

Q11 *Chocolat*

Q12 *Titanic*

Q13 *Home Alone*

Q14 *I Am Sam*

Q15 B

Cryptic crossword 4

Circuit 5

Q1 A (maharaja, flapjack)

Q2 A flying sorcerer

Q3

3	3	6	9
15	24	39	63
102	165	267	432

Q4 Raquel Welch

Q5 vice, vile, pile, pole, polo, solo

Q6

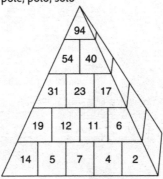

Q7

9	1	2	3	5	8	4	7	6
3	4	7	1	2	6	5	8	9
5	6	8	4	7	9	1	2	3
1	2	4	5	3	7	6	9	8
6	5	3	8	9	1	2	4	7
7	8	9	2	6	4	3	1	5
2	7	6	9	4	3	8	5	1
4	3	1	7	8	5	9	6	2
8	9	5	6	1	2	7	3	4

Q8   360
Q9   64
Q10 14
Q11 *Forrest Gump*
Q12 *Les Misérables*
Q13 *Blowup*
Q14 *Erin Brockovich* (B.Rock.O.Vic.H)
Q15 A

Cryptic crossword 5

Circuit 6

Q1 £300 i.e. 300 minus (150 + 10) leaves £140, minus (70 + 10) leaves £60 minus (30 + 10) = £40, leaves £20 from original £300.

Q2 Minimum

Q3 Only the 1st

Q4 Barbara Carrera

Q5 deck, beck, back, bask, bass, boss

Q6

132				
61	71			
28	33	38		
13	15	18	20	
5	8	7	11	9

Q7

1	4	2	3	5	7	6	8	9
3	6	8	1	2	9	7	4	5
5	7	9	4	6	8	1	2	3
2	1	3	5	8	4	9	7	6
4	8	5	7	9	6	2	3	1
6	9	7	2	1	3	4	5	8
7	5	1	6	3	2	8	9	4
9	2	6	8	4	5	3	1	7
8	3	4	9	7	1	5	6	2

Cryptic crossword 6

Circuit 7

Q1 Elucidate

Q2 Kidney

Q3

2	4	1				1	4	3
	2	4	5		8	5	9	
		5	6	4	3	7		
			7	6	9			
				8				
			6	2	9			
		4	8	9	6	7		
	2	8	9		3	8	9	
4	9	7				9	3	5

Q4 Kim Basinger

Q5 sank, sand, said, skid, skim, swim

Q6

78	59	15	21	46
13	17	108	69	12
63	20	19	66	51
23	43	62	43	48
42	80	15	20	62

Q7

1	3	4	2	5	6	8	7	9
6	5	9	1	7	8	2	3	4
7	2	8	3	4	9	1	5	6
5	1	6	4	8	3	7	9	2
2	4	3	5	9	7	6	1	8
8	9	7	6	1	2	3	4	5
3	8	5	7	2	4	9	6	1
9	6	1	8	3	5	4	2	7
4	7	2	9	6	1	5	8	3

Q8 180
Q9 50
Q10 11
Q11 *(Three Colours) Red, White (and) Blue*
Q12 *Castaway*
Q13 *(The) Godfather*
Q14 *Psycho*
Q15 F

Cryptic crossword 7

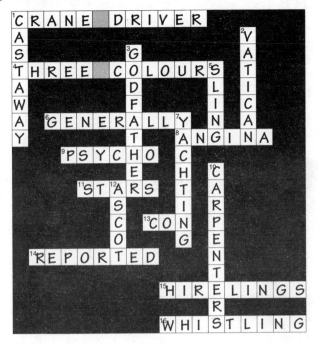

Circuit 8

Q1   52 (double the sum of the first two numbers in the row)

Q2   Parole

Q3   On 21 November

Q4   Debbie Harry

Q5   foot, font, fond, bond, band, hand

Q6

46	59	12	38	81
4	43	130	51	8
74	25	14	69	54
46	47	66	47	30
66	62	14	31	63

Q7

1	2	4	5	6	7	9	8	3
3	5	7	1	9	8	2	4	6
6	8	9	2	4	3	5	7	1
2	1	6	3	7	4	8	5	9
4	3	5	8	1	9	6	2	7
7	9	8	6	2	5	3	1	4
8	4	3	9	5	1	7	6	2
9	6	1	7	8	2	4	3	5
5	7	2	4	3	6	1	9	8

Q8 147
Q9 42
Q10 9
Q11 *Amélie*
Q12 *(The French) Connection*
Q13 *The Hours*
Q14 *The Apartment*
Q15 C

Cryptic crossword 8

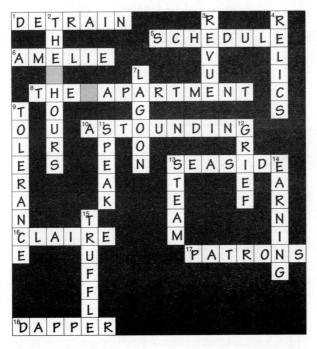

Circuit 9

Q1 Mora Mora £3.00, Sambirano £3.60

Q2 Shotgun

Q3

1	2	3	4	5	6	7	8	9	10	11	12	13	14	15	16	17	18	19	20	21
T	A	B	L	E	S	I	O	N	T	A	R	I	O	W	N	E	U	R	O	N

Q4 Christie Brinkley

Q5 beer, beet, belt, bell, bill, mill, milk

Q6

33	10	52	36	59
32	60	47	38	13
24	98	18	38	12
42	16	29	38	65
59	6	44	40	41

Q7

8	6	2	1	4	5	7	3	9
5	1	3	7	9	6	4	2	8
4	7	9	8	2	3	5	1	6
9	5	8	3	7	4	2	6	1
7	2	1	6	5	9	3	8	4
3	4	6	2	1	8	9	5	7
6	3	7	9	8	2	1	4	5
2	9	5	4	6	1	8	7	3
1	8	4	5	3	7	6	9	2

Q8 144
Q9 40
Q10 7
Q11 *MASH*
Q12 *Citizen Kane*
Q13 *Howards End*
Q14 *The Piano*
Q15 B

Cryptic crossword 9

Circuit 10

Q1 Lean ('jogging up' the word 'lane' produces 'lean' (anagram) meaning reduced fat)

Q2 Illegal

Q3 C

Q4 Pamela Stephenson

Q5 toad, goad, glad, clad, clod, clog, flog, frog

Q6

44	24	28	24	22
30	8	37	28	39
25	32	26	36	23
25	48	19	28	22
18	30	32	26	36

Q7

1	2	3	4	5	7	6	9	8
5	4	9	1	6	8	2	7	3
6	7	8	2	3	9	1	4	5
2	1	5	3	9	6	4	8	7
3	8	6	7	1	4	5	2	9
4	9	7	5	8	2	3	6	1
7	3	2	8	4	5	9	1	6
8	6	1	9	2	3	7	5	4
9	5	4	6	7	1	8	3	2

Q8 108
Q9 39
Q10 6
Q11 *La Dolce Vita*
Q12 *Dirty Dancing*
Q13 *The Dirty Dozen*
Q14 *Billy Elliot*
Q15 H

Cryptic crossword 10

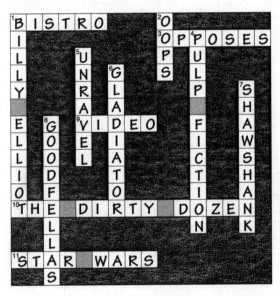

Circuit 11

Q1 Theology
Q2 walkie-talkie
Q3 Missing number is 728. (648 − 284) 5 2 = 728.
Q4 Jaclyn Smith
Q5 tree, thee, them, teem, team, tear, pear
Q6

25	24	5	21	43
6	41	63	5	3
27	27	8	19	37
21	23	37	23	14
39	3	5	50	21

Q7

1	2	4	3	5	6	8	7	9
5	6	7	1	8	9	2	3	4
9	3	8	2	4	7	1	5	6
2	1	3	4	6	8	5	9	7
6	4	5	9	7	2	3	8	1
7	8	9	5	1	3	4	6	2
8	9	1	7	2	5	6	4	3
4	7	6	8	3	1	9	2	5
3	5	2	6	9	4	7	1	8

Q8 100
Q9 37
Q10 5
Q11 *East Is East*
Q12 *(Bend It) like Beckham*
Q13 *Dr. Strangelove*
Q14 *The Graduate*
Q15 C

Cryptic crossword 11

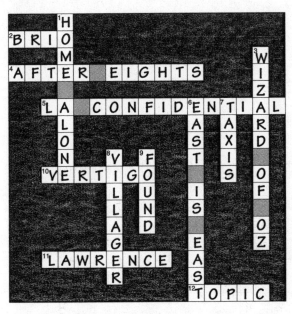

Circuit 12

Q1 Transcontinental
Q2 Whatever
Q3

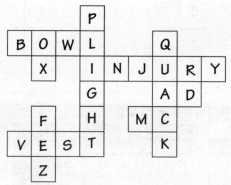

Q4 Isabella Rossellini
Q5 read, road, rood, rook, book
Q6

20	14	28	23	26
17	30	36	22	6
9	50	13	24	15
29	14	8	22	38
36	3	26	20	26

Q7

1	2	3	4	7	5	6	9	8
4	5	6	9	1	8	2	3	7
7	8	9	2	6	3	1	5	4
2	1	4	8	3	9	7	6	5
3	6	7	1	5	2	4	8	9
5	9	8	6	4	7	3	1	2
6	3	2	5	8	4	9	7	1
9	7	5	3	2	1	8	4	6
8	4	1	7	9	6	5	2	3

Q8 90
Q9 24
Q10 4
Q11 *Cabaret*
Q12 *Philadelphia*
Q13 *(To Kill a) Mockingbird*
Q14 *Rain Man*
Q15 C

Cryptic crossword 12

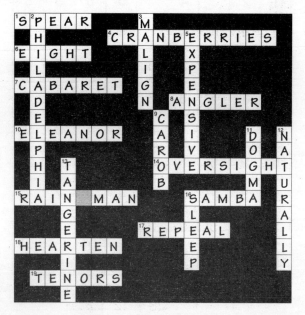

Circuit 13

Q1 The five letters can make S N A I L (as in 'at a snail's pace').

Q2 Box Brownie

Q3

S	H	A	V	E
H	A	V	E	N
A	V	E	R	T
V	E	R	S	E
E	N	T	E	R

Q4 Elle Macpherson

Q5 coin, corn, cord, cold, gold

Q6

31	4	23	12	21
23	12	9	18	29
10	38	11	22	10
10	24	27	18	12
17	13	21	21	19

Q7

1	9	2	3	4	5	6	7	8
3	4	5	6	7	8	2	1	9
6	7	8	1	2	9	3	4	5
5	3	7	4	8	6	1	9	2
2	1	6	7	9	3	5	8	4
4	8	9	2	5	1	7	6	3
7	2	1	8	3	4	9	5	6
9	6	4	5	1	2	8	3	7
8	5	3	9	6	7	4	2	1

Q8 87
Q9 23
Q10 3
Q11 *(The) Sound of Music*
Q12 *The Third Man*
Q13 *The Sting*
Q14 *(The) African Queen*
Q15 D

Cryptic crossword 13

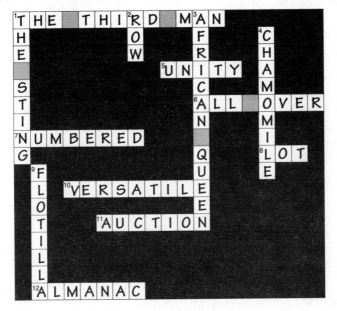

Circuit 14

Q1 sheep, sheen, shell, sheath
Q2 A website
Q3

1	2	3	4	5	6	7	8	9	10	11	12	13	14	15	16	17	18	19	20	21	22	23	24
V	I	N	O	R	S	C	A	M	N	E	S	I	A	N	S	W	E	R	N	I	C	K	E

Q4 Madonna
Q5 camp, came, same, sate, site
Q6

23	15	16	7	17
4	15	19	25	15
5	22	8	38	5
33	15	11	5	14
13	11	24	3	27

Q7

2	3	4	6	5	7	8	1	9
1	5	7	2	8	9	3	4	6
6	9	8	1	3	4	2	5	7
3	1	2	4	7	6	5	9	8
5	7	9	3	2	8	1	6	4
4	8	6	5	9	1	7	2	3
7	2	1	9	6	3	4	8	5
8	6	5	7	4	2	9	3	1
9	4	3	8	1	5	6	7	2

Q8 80
Q9 22
Q10 2
Q11 *Unforgiven*
Q12 *Lassie*
Q13 *ET*
Q14 *The Lion King*
Q15 A

Cryptic crossword 14

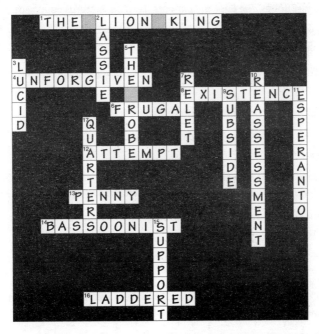

Taking it further

Recommended reading

A.R. Damasio, 'Neuropathology of emotion and mood', *Nature* 386 (1997), pp. 768–70.

T. Glynne-Jones, *The Book of Numbers* (London: Arcturus Foulsham, 2007).

F. Greeff, *The Hidden Code of Cryptic Crosswords* (East Dereham, UK: Foulsham, 2003).

S.A. Greenfield, *The Human Brain: A Guided Tour* (London: Weidenfeld & Nicolson, 1997).

S. Gupta, 'Brawn and Brain', in *Time magazine* (May 2004).

T. Horne and S. Wootton, *Train Your Brain* (London: Hodder Education, 2010).

P.J. Howard, *The Owner's Manual for the Brain: Everyday Applications from Mind and Brain Research*, 3rd edn (Austin, TX: Bard Press, 2006).

E. Kandel et al. (eds), *Principles of Neural Science*, 4th edn (New York: McGraw Hill, 2000).

M.-M. Mesulam, *Principles of Behavioural and Cognitive Neurology*, 2nd edn (New York: OUP, 2000).

S.R. Quartz and T.J. Sejnowski, *Liars, Lovers and Heroes* (New York: Harper Collins, 2002).

I. Robertson, *Mind Sculpture* (New York: Bantam Books, 1999).

I. Robertson, *Stay Sharp with the Mind Doctor* (London: Vermilion, 2005).

M. Rosenzweig, 'Effects of training in adult brains', *Brain Behaviour Research* 18 (1996), pp. 56–66.

K. Schaie, *Intellectual Development in Adulthood: The Seattle Longitudinal Study* (Cambridge: Cambridge University Press, 1996).

J. Victoroff, *Saving Your Brain: The Revolutionary Plan to Boost Brain Power, Improve Memory, and Protect Yourself against Aging and Alzheimer's* (New York: Bantam Books, 2002).

S. Wooton and T. Horne, *Strategic Thinking* (London: Kogan Page, 2005).

Websites

www.brainwaves.com (Look for 'Building mental muscle and left brain power' by A. Bragdon and D. Gamon; also 'A photo quiz for the mind's eye'.)

Image credits